TOSCANINI
and
Great Music

by Lawrence Gilman

WAGNER'S OPERAS

TOSCANINI AND GREAT MUSIC

ARTURO TOSCANINI

TOSCANINI
and
Great Music

By

LAWRENCE GILMAN
Music Critic of
The New York Herald Tribune
and
AUTHOR OF "WAGNER'S OPERAS"

FARRAR & RINEHART
INCORPORATED
New York *Toronto*

To
E. W. G.

CONTENTS

AUTHOR'S NOTE

IT is a pleasure for me to avow, at the beginning of this book, an unpayable debt of gratitude to that valiant idealist, David Sarnoff, for having conceived and effected the restoration of Toscanini to the musical life of America—a debt which I share with millions of other music lovers on this continent. My colleague, Samuel Chotzinoff, whose coöperative tact, wisdom, and devotion equipped him as ambassador extraordinary in the successful accomplishment of a difficult task, has likewise earned my gratitude for his part in that formidable enterprise.

I am obligated to an indulgent friend on holiday, Miss Gertrude Wolf, for her sacrificial labors in making the index for this book when she should have been enjoying her vacation.

Mrs. Helen Herbert, of Sugar Hill, New Hampshire, has given me indispensable aid by her

AUTHOR'S NOTE

diligence and skill in transforming my dishevelled handwriting into presentable typescript.

❀   ❀   ❀

I have been privileged by Messrs. G. P. Putnam's Sons, American publishers of Karel Capek's book, *The Gardener's Year,* to use the excerpt from that delectable masterpiece which appears in my final chapter, "The Music Lover." Alfred A. Knopf, Inc., have generously permitted me to avail myself of passages from the late J. W. N. Sullivan's *Beethoven: His Spiritual Development* (New York, 1927). I have quoted from the *Life of Ludwig van Beethoven,* by Alexander Wheelock Thayer, edited and revised by Henry Edward Krehbiel (published by The Beethoven Association, New York, through G. Schirmer, Inc., 1927); and from Sir Donald Francis Tovey's unrivalled *Essays in Musical Analysis* (Oxford University Press, 1935-1937).

PREFACE

THIS is not a biography of Toscanini. There are other books that deal with Toscanini the man. I am not here concerned with Toscanini's career, nor with his personality as a human being, but rather with his quality as a musician. I have tried to set down the reasons why Toscanini, the re-creative artist, seems to me to be unique. I have wanted to make clearer, so far as that is possible, the ways in which his conducting illuminates some of the music that he interprets, and is in turn illuminated by the greatness of the works themselves. This is a book about Toscanini the priest of music, and about certain masterworks that he reveals, and the significance of their interaction for the democratic culture of our time.

❦ ❦ ❦

The soundest definition of what one means by a cultivated mind is probably the most familiar:

[xi]

PREFACE

To know the best that has been thought and said
in the world. For more years than one likes to
think, that famous definition was not generally as-
sumed to include the art of music; probably because
most of the intellectuals of the world—the men of
letters, scientists, philosophers, historians—were
imperfectly aware of the fact that music is a
major art, as well as a species of entertainment.

But that assumption has changed, not because
the men of letters, scientists, philosophers, and historians themselves have changed (the name of Beethoven is absent from the best-known modern history of civilization), but because a change is being
forced upon them by the average man. Within the
last decade or so the average man has discovered,
chiefly through the agency of phonograph record-
ings and radio broadcasts, that the art of music is
not the province of a few incomprehensible spe-
cialists, but a vast and boundless continent of the
mind, inexhaustible in its riches for the spirit.

Mr. Bernard Shaw once observed that "the
truth is the funniest thing in the world." It is also,
in many cases, the most surprising thing in the
world. The truth that was evidently discerned by
the National Broadcasting Company when it engaged the most fanatically uncompromising of mu-

sical idealists to direct the undertaking which it has brought to a peak of unexampled popular success was a no less surprising one than this: that the growth of the popular appetite for the experiences that great music has to offer is neither a delusion nor a hope nor a dream. It is an actuality, already obvious to the more perceptive among the realistic and the practical, increasingly suspected by others. Great beauty, supreme excellence, have become factors in our contemporary living that are no longer wisely to be ignored. They have become, in many instances, the most profitable things in music, in the theatre, in art, in the films.

It is being demonstrated by and to innumerable listeners that the bravest idealism and the loftiest faith are not only the most exciting and absorbing things in this disintegrating world, but the most substantial and secure—that nothing else is comparatively rewarding and dependable.

Our terrestrial habitation is not, at present, the happiest of places; yet there is a spirit abroad today, among those who remain potentially or actually civilized, that is full of a new intensity and eagerness, that hungers and thirsts after the beauty and greatness of imponderable things. It was the most satirical and tough-minded of living thinkers

PREFACE

who wrote not long ago: "I am receiving every scientific statement with dour suspicion, whilst giving very respectful consideration to the inspiration and revelations of the prophets and poets."

Toscanini is among the foremost of the prophets and poets of that subliminal world of indestructible beauty and reality that lies so near our own. He is no visionary who has merely slept and dreamed there: he is creatively alive there, an active instrument of revelation. He brings about us not "its fallen day," but its continuing reality of fidelity and faith and inspiration, so that we see, if only for a moment, the truth as it really is, overwhelming in clarity and splendor. L. G.

SUGAR HILL,
NEW HAMPSHIRE,
July 5, 1938.

TOSCANINI
and
Great Music

I

THE MUSIC BEHIND THE NOTES

"IF WE should see the sun for the first time," remarked the alleviating Mr. Chesterton, "it would seem to us the most fearful and beautiful of meteors. Now that we see it for the thousandth time, we call it, in the hideous and blasphemous phrase of Wordsworth, 'the light of common day.'"

I have tried in these pages to pay tribute to a great and singular musician who in all the half-century that he has been conducting orchestras has never looked upon a masterpiece of music without seeing it as though for the first time, and being penetrated and possessed anew by its greatness. I think it is one of the things that might be said of the supreme interpreter that he is a re-creative artist who has not wearied of wonders. For what is the distinguishing characteristic of such an artist but that ability of his to give us the sense of quickened and quickening con-

[3]

tact with familiar works? Other signs betray his presence: but that is the unmistakable and certain signal.

❦   ❦   ❦

It is thirty years—a generation, as some would reckon—since Arturo Toscanini, then in his forty-second year, first came to the United States. Since that evening when he made his debut at the Metropolitan—the date was November 16, 1908, the opera *Aïda*—he has been a figure of increasing influence and unique distinction in the experience of those Americans who care most deeply for that which is rarest in musical art. His departure from the Metropolitan in 1915 and his return to Italy; his visit here in the winter of 1920-21 for a concert tour with the orchestra of La Scala; his first appearance in 1926 with what is now the Philharmonic-Symphony, his unforgettable achievements with that orchestra, and his resignation in 1936; his return to New York in December, 1937, to take charge of the newly-formed symphony orchestra of the National Broadcasting Company, and the unexampled weekly concerts of that organization under his direction which have given a new extension and significance to our ideas concerning the democratization of musical culture—

[4]

these events are milestones in the musical history of America.

How often, especially in these later years of Toscanini's association with symphonic music in America, his return has been looked upon as the cardinal event of the musical season in New York! How long, and how affectionately, New Yorkers have known that familiar and characteristic ritual of inauguration—the packed, expectant, audience-room; the resolute emergence of the vigorous, sturdy figure with the countenance of legendary beauty and nobility and the burning deep-set eyes; the progress, with bent head, across the stage to the podium, as though the walker hoped to reach the conductor's stand without being noticed; the rising orchestra and audience, and the irrepressible outburst of welcome and salutation; the prompt dispatch of the unavoidable business of greeting and acknowledgment, and the turning to his players; the sharp, imperative rap of the stick upon a near-by violin-desk; the immediate assumption of mysterious authority and control by a magnetizing will over a hundred other wills; and the release of a beauty and clarity and precision of orchestral sound which made it evident that Toscanini had returned.

Now, three decades after he first came to the

[5]

United States, Toscanini, a prodigy of youthful re-
silience and strength and endurance, an even more
vital and compelling artist than before, has returned
to us again, and one may hear the First Musician
of the world conduct symphonic music broadcast by
an orchestra established and supported for no other
purpose than that he should make of it a perfected
vehicle for the widest possible diffusion of great
music; and these concerts enter the receiving sets
of who shall say how many million homes?

It is human to take the marvellous for granted.
Yet for some of us who live among the material
conquests of the modern age, it seems less wonderful that men should have made both space and time
fictitious than that they should still trust to the po-
tentiality of ideal things in a world that grows more
and more ferocious.

The daring adventure of the National Broadcasting Company in bringing Toscanini back to
America and building an orchestra for his special
use is an outcome of the conviction that fine symphonic music and great symphonic leadership are
immensely and increasingly popular in America;
and if that does not amount to putting trust in the
power of ideal things, how, then, should one describe it?

Apparently this faith is justified. That careful and weariless student of living fact, the lordly magazine *Fortune,* has informed us that the answers to a recent national survey including "questions concerning radios, musical programs, and the name of Arturo Toscanini," showed that "more than half of the United States" likes to listen to good music; and that "of all the people in the United States—farmers, clerks, Negroes, poor whites, and millionaires"—more than a fourth know who Toscanini is and what he does.

Perhaps it is scarcely to be wondered at, therefore, that the NBC is said to have received approximately 50,000 requests for tickets of admission to the broadcast studio in which the Italian master and his ninety-odd musicians gave their first concert under his direction on the night of Christmas, 1937. Yet it should be borne in mind that these NBC Symphony concerts under Toscanini are not to be regarded as concerts given for the benefit of listeners in the room where they originate. That is not at all their purpose or their function. They are given primarily for wireless transmission to those who are listening before receiving sets. Logically considered, they do not exist as concerts in a hall.

Of course it is regrettable that so many persons who become aware of Toscanini's power as an interpreter of music must forgo the experience of seeing him in action—an experience that has its own legitimate and undeniable fascination for the appreciative musician no less than for the casual concertgoer. But for those who are sufficiently well served by their receiving sets, and sufficiently perceptive to know what beautiful and realizing sound the conductor and his players are achieving, these concerts become wholly and sufficingly an experience of the ear and the kindled imagination and the spirit quickened and released.

❀   ❀   ❀

Toscanini's fame is probably without parallel in the annals of music: not because its extent and its reverberations have no precedent, but because celebrity such as he has won had never come to an artist of his kind. For bear in mind that Toscanini is the least sensational of music-makers. To think of him as a "star," a "virtuoso"—using those words with all the connotations that they traditionally carry—would be the most grotesque of misconceptions.

Everything that is commonly implied and sug-

gested by those dubious terms is astronomically remote from the nature and the ways of this unassum-
ing artist, who has never attempted to lure the favor
of the public—who has never won it, indeed, save
as it can be won through uncompromising aesthetic
rectitude, and an intensity of devotional fervor incomprehensible to the worldly and the overwise.

That a musician so wholly unpretentious, moving habitually in the loftiest regions of the musical
imagination, should have become the idol of a public of many millions, restores one's faith in the re-
sistless power of spiritual greatness. Such power,
clearly, is a function of that mysterious order of
illumination which, we have been told, exists im-
mutably, known by all, in some measure, through
fitness or through grace: an illumination so pene-
trating that it brings the sense of order and beauty
to those who have it as well as to those who need
it most—"the proud, the brave, the gentle, and the
blind."

And thus the attitude of the musical public in
its relation to this artist remains one of the major
validations of our period and our race.

There have been some, no doubt, who were
drawn to Toscanini for other and more superficial

reasons, since an artist so exceptional could scarcely help being, despite himself, a sensational apparition. Yet many of those who came to gape and chatter have remained to be subdued by a simplicity and devoutness obvious at last to all.

❧   ❧   ❧

Those of us who love music, and seek to derive from it all that it can give us of fulfillment and release, should remind ourselves now and again of the inestimable service that such artists as Toscanini render through their exalted devotion to the masters whose greatness they make part of our experience. I think we should realize what it is that Toscanini has meant to us during the years that he has spent here as a vehicle of revelation, and what he means increasingly to those who are now able to receive his benefactions. We who have heard him oftenest, and have known him, as an artist, longest and best, should give our evidence. In later years, what we know to be the truth about him will not be believed. It will survive as a legend and a myth, a fable scarcely conceivable as fact. Let us admit that even now, today and in the present, the truth concerning such an artist passes the bounds of credibility.

What is it, then, that this extraordinary artist signifies? Let us try to see him as he has always been since he first came here, and as he remains today—the weariless, fanatical perfectionist who cares with so preposterous an intensity for the ideal of beauty and excellence which torments him that saner minds, content with easier ways, can but shake their heads over his apparent madness and his evident self-torture.

Toscanini is remarkable in many ways; but in nothing is he so remarkable as in his possession of what a statesman of other days called a one-track mind. In Toscanini's mind, this single track is that which runs between his conception of an ideal excellence and its possible realization. For him it is a one-way route, without sidings, without branches. The inflexible purpose that moves so irresistibly along this aesthetic road is not to be diverted. If there is an obstacle ahead, it is the obstacle that suffers, not the flamelike purpose and the steellike will.

This tireless quest for an inaccessible perfection is seldom so unswervingly pursued as it is in Toscanini's case. Many artists who follow their own conceptions of excellence and beauty are willing to indulge themselves in humanities and relaxations and resting places along the way. For Toscanini, such things are not merely ignored: they simply do not exist. There are the love and absorption of the votary, the religious humility of the priest before the sacrament; there is the vision of the artist, his dream of an unattainable rectitude; and there is the possible route to its accomplishment. These are the only factors in the case, so far as Toscanini is concerned. There is nothing else.

His conducting is almost an act of desperation. It is evident that Toscanini's inward ear is constantly echoing with a justness and purity of disembodied sound for which there are no wholly satisfying vehicles in this imperfect world of all-too-human players upon material instruments. Is it to be wondered at that such interpreters can never be quite happy? Living among rarefied, essential things, their patience is easily exhausted by intervening substances, media that are stubborn and obstructive. Their own world, ablaze with mysteriously lucid fires, is far more real than the known universe about them. In the midst of death they are in life. They are wakeners, desperately hopeful. Dwelling at the center of the spirit's clearest vision, they agonize over the pulselessness of all beloved things.

❀ ❀ ❀

Toscanini unconsciously reminds us that only those artists can touch the deepest springs who manifest their single-mindedness, their purity of intention, their incorruptible sincerity. It is their special relation to their task that stirs and persuades us.

We perceive, first, their high seriousness—that fine, unchallengeable seriousness which springs from absolute sincerity. Always they give us a curious sense of consecration—of dedication and self-effacement. They are anything but self-conscious or self-important as they draw aside the veil or raise the chalice. They could not be: for they are thinking neither of us nor of themselves, but of that which they would fain become: interpreters of an art that they would set before us in its completeness and reality: vehicles of revelation: torches to be lit at an everlasting flame.

Toscanini has given us again and again this sense of absorbed and self-forgetful dedication, and of that which follows in its train when the artist is an interpreter of genius: that sense of deep and complete identification with his subject.

The faculty of imaginative re-creation is not to be explained. How are its results accomplished? By surpassing insight and consummate art, one might reply. But when one has said that, one has said nothing; for the mysteries of the re-creative imagination begin at the point where words falter and desert us.

No interpreter can give us the sense of imaginative identification without that mysterious, inexhaustible vitality of the will and spirit, the quickening touch, which Toscanini has.

A subtle and profound philosopher has reminded us that the essential quality of poetry is that it be truly lived in the spirit of the singer; that it be, indeed, the living word. Artists such as Toscanini give us this lived and living word. Thoreau, that chief imaginative genius of America, great woodsman, great seer, has said that "at first blush a man is not capable of reporting truth; he must be drenched and saturated with it first. It will be necessary that he be in a sense translated in order to understand the truth. . . . It is, indeed, a rare qualification," he added, "to be able to conceive and

[14]

suffer the truth to pass through us living and intact."

To conceive and suffer the truth to pass through one living and intact: that is what great music, or great drama, asks of the interpreter. Thus, what sets the interpreter of genius permanently apart is that he gives us, in his conveyance of great art—a symphony, a song, a character in drama—not a mere approximation, but what we recognize with certainty as the full embodiment of the creator's thought. This, we say, is not a singer telling us what Schubert thought of Death in one of its eternal aspects; this is the awe and mystery and gentleness of Death itself as Schubert felt it. Or, as we realize when Toscanini sets before us the C minor Symphony of Beethoven, this is the recovered voice of the creator, speaking to us of valor and enormous struggle and unconquerable strength, and the glory and release of victory.

❧   ❧   ❧

The greatness of a work of art is no guarantee, alas, that it will always speak to us with its proper and essential voice. Great music is not staled and withered by custom or by age so much as by the intermediation of inferior interpreters. There are some who maintain that music is independent of the great interpreter: that the interpreter (the conductor in this case) is needed only for the purpose of directing the music's course and keeping it in order, as though he were a traffic policeman of the aural art; and that any such policeman is good enough for the purpose.

But that is a fallacy. The secrets of music do not lie open to the mastery of any conductor who chooses to peer into its baffling eyes. The blunt truth is that only a great conductor can read them or impart them. We are not hearing Beethoven's C minor Symphony in its completeness when we hear it at the hands of an average conductor. We may think we are, but that is a delusion.

Beethoven and Brahms and Wagner cannot speak to us unless they are aided by those who are worthy to convey their greatness. Like the dead in Maeterlinck's affecting fable, they come to life only when the living think of them: and in that art whose essence is re-creation, none but the life-givers truly live.

All music that is worth the mystical and agonizing process of re-creation can be fully released from its casing of symbols only by those choice and singular artists who bring to it the paradoxical blend of imperious will and profound humility which the great interpreter exhibits. It is true that the great interpreter, like other artists of genius, is sometimes, in the performance of his task, relentless, dictatorial, inconsiderate. He must be. Yet observe him as he liberates the *Eroica* or the Ninth—observe him then, and it is possible that you may ever afterward think of him not as despotic and inhuman, but as brother to the knight "who has knelt through his long office, and who has the piety of his office."

❀   ❀   ❀

On the occasion of Toscanini's first visit to London as a symphonic conductor, Bernard Shaw interrogated an American friend of the Maestro's who was in London at the time. "Tell me something about this man Toscanini," said the waggish Mr. Shaw. "Is he sober, honest, and industrious?"

Mr. Shaw, doubtless without suspecting it, had chosen the precisely descriptive words for certain of Toscanini's salient attributes as an artist. Toscanini's sobriety, his honesty, and his industry as a re-creative artist—plus the thing that we merely thrust further into its mysterious background by calling it "genius"—are conspicuous among his traits. He is the final retort to the popular conception of the great conductor as necessarily something of an exhibitionist and trimmer. The "effect," the compromise, the easier way, are inconceivably distant from the procedures of this unusual artist.

His relation to the work in hand is always his one and exclusive concern. His self-imposed demand for the utmost possible fidelity, the most arduous and unsparing concentration of endeavor, is never abated. He has that unshakable faith of the rare artist in the sufficient rewardingness of the last full measure of devotion that he brings to his task of re-creation. Among one's engaging memories of Toscanini's preoccupations at a European festival is that of his weariless patience and industry in tracking down the authority for what he suspected to be an erroneous dynamic marking in all the editions of one of Wagner's scores. Relatively viewed, it was a minor point; but for Toscanini there are no minor points in connection with a work of art, and the correct dynamic marking of a single note is no less devotedly to be established than the governing tempo of the *Parsifal* Prelude or the rhythmic definition of Siegfried's Funeral Hymn.

Toscanini, an incorrigibly modest man, honestly

self-deprecating, would probably say that the quickening of lifeless symbols upon a page of music is only a matter of executing with the maximum fidelity the composer's recorded wishes. Yet any conscientious, intelligent, scrupulous, attentive, and practiced routinier, as barren of re-creative imagination as the stick between his fingers, can execute the composer's written orders—so far as they are definitely ascertainable, which is by no means always the case.

But to execute faithfully what is written on the page is but the beginning of the re-creator's task. That sort of fidelity is the first of the interpreter's necessary virtues, but it is only the first. To his scrupulous observance of the notes, the great interpreter, by virtue of the power that his genius gives him, adds "the unimaginable touch," the reality behind the notes: the music of which the notes are but the crude approximation. He ceases to be merely the devoted literalist, and becomes the inexplicable life-giver, the master of a secret vision and an incommunicable speech, known only to himself and to his peers. He becomes, unconsciously, possessed and possessing. He becomes, in that most debased and most vulgarized and most sublime of words, inspired: "breathing from a greater self than his own and telling more truth than he knew."

Yet there are few musical fallacies more respectable and hoary than that to which I have alluded: the fallacy that a conductor, aside from discharging a few obvious and elementary functions, need merely, in the sanctified phrase, "let the music speak for itself." Every once in a while an artist of exceptional imaginative insight and kindling power comes before us and makes nonsense of this hallowed thesis; but that is apparently of no concern to the lovers of unexamined formulas, who continue to reiterate with solemn assurance what every clear-minded observer knows is an absurdity.

      ✿   ✿   ✿

Perhaps the greatest service in the cause of aesthetic enlightenment achieved by Toscanini in the years of his conductorship among us has been his conspicuous demonstration of the falsity of this deluding and harmful theory. Of course the theory is also invalidated on every occasion that an earnest and efficient mediocrity confronts a masterpiece and attempts the pious task of "letting the music speak for itself"; for we are invariably, on such occasions, made aware of the difference between sterility and creation—between the lifeless performance that we cannot remember and the fecundating performance that we cannot forget. But negative demonstrations of this sort are quietly ignored by all save aesthetic realists.

It might be supposed, however, that the sort of positive demonstration afforded us time after time by Toscanini would have given its deathblow to the fond, enfeebled doctrine of the self-sufficiency of masterworks. But the old belief dies hard, and it is reasserted whenever a favorable opportunity is presented for the triumphant exhibition of critical obscurantism.

"He was a wise statesman," remarked an historian concerning an eminent figure of the past, "and so sound on most economic theories that his party . . . refused him recognition for nearly a quarter of a century." We can scarcely say that Toscanini has been refused recognition, since he is the most illustrious conductor who ever lived; but it is a fact that one of his exceptional gifts as an artist—his power of revelation and re-creation—has not been recognized by some of those who should have been the first to perceive and acclaim it. The history of criticism in our era will surely note with something like incredulity the remarkable circumstance that at the close of one of Toscanini's seasons here, during which he had accomplished prodigies in the disclosure of unsuspected values in familiar scores, he was said by a responsible authority to have "achieved no revelations of well-known masterworks"—a statement that was entirely true, except for the fact that the little word "no" did not belong there.

What have come to be known as conductor's "readings" are another matter altogether. "Readings," in the commonly accepted and opprobrious sense of the term, are willfully individualistic conceptions of familiar masterworks, fashioned for the ulterior purpose of magnifying the interpreter at the expense of the interpreted. From such displays of exhibitionism, sincere and sensitive music lovers and musicians will always turn with repugnance and disdain. But I am discussing an artist, not a charlatan.

The great conductor does not seek to add anything extraneous to the music that he takes in hand. His only aim is to draw forth, illuminate. He is unreservedly and humbly at the service of the composer and his thought. He does not willfully alter or exploit; he interprets.

And what, in this sense, does the verb "interpret" mean? Let us, for a moment, consult that faithful friend of man, the Dictionary:

"Interpret, *v:* To give objective representation of, as the work of a composer . . . To unfold, make clear, elucidate."

Objective representation—clarification—elucidation—unfolding: those are justly descriptive words for an inexplicable process.

❦　　❦　　❦

I have said that such interpreters as Toscanini do not deliberately add anything extraneous to Beethoven or Brahms or Wagner; and that is true. But despite the wish of the interpreter, something necessarily is added to the composer, and that is the interpreter himself, for the simple reason that he cannot be removed from the equation. Music never has "spoken for itself," and never will, because it cannot. If it is music for an orchestra, it can speak only through the conductor, by way of the hundred or so executants whose wills and imaginations he must bend and kindle, so that they will share and transmit his own conception of the meaning of the patterned notes.

This is true not merely in the bald and obvious sense that music is nothing but written symbols until it is translated into sound. It is true also in the more searching and deeper sense that there is no way by which we may get at the composer except through the interpreter. That interpreter may be oneself, alone in the silence of one's library, studying the score, or renewing an ancient friendship with its symbols and the imagined reality behind them. It may be the conductor plus his hundred men. But the interpreter, whoever he may be, is inescapable. It is *his* account of Beethoven or Brahms or Wagner or Debussy that you will always and inevitably get. For those pitiful great phantoms are inarticulate; nor have they guiding hands that they can lay upon us. They are eternally imprisoned in the mystery and remoteness of their own protean beauty, which is changeless, yet infinitely changeable, besought by all men for a sign, but yielding its secrets only to a few who are supremely choice and fit. What is the Dirge of the *Eroica* until some life-giver such as Toscanini has quickened its "giant heart of memory and tears"? Thereafter it dies, and is a legend, until another quickener summons it again to life. For every great performance is a resurrection, and he who achieves it is a worker of miracles.

❦   ❦   ❦

It is odd how reluctant many persons are to admit that an interpreting artist may become creative through his ability to animate and transfigure the lifeless symbols of recorded music. The written notes of the B minor Mass or the Ninth Symphony are not the Mass or the Symphony: they are only directions left by Bach and Beethoven for the guidance of conductors and instrumentalists and singers. A composer makes signs with ink or with pencil on ruled paper, and these are preserved for us by the engraver and the printing press. A month, a year, a century later, some fiddler, pianist, singer, or conductor, studying the composer's necessarily skeletonized outline of that which his imagination had conceived and wrought, derives from it a pattern of organized, significant sound. The skeleton assumes the beauty and the warmth of living flesh, the lifeless notes put on that fugitive, recurrent immortality which is the unique estate of music among the arts, and the familiar marvel is achieved.

If this amazing process is not worthy to be

called "creation"—if this is not a bringing into life of that which was no more the living reality of music than "s-u-n" is the living, recurrent miracle of light and warmth—then our terms of recognition and of praise are in need of drastic overhauling. Yet criticism has been satisfied to call Flotow or Godard or Ambroise Thomas a "creative artist," and Toscanini or Heifetz or Casals a mere "interpreter," praised, in that least examined of all critical clichés, for "letting the music speak for itself": which is as if one had paid tribute to Bernhardt for letting the role of Phèdre "speak for itself."

"How very anxious Reynolds is," exclaimed Blake, "to disprove or contemn spiritual perception!" It sometimes seems as if incompletely reflective musicians were actuated by a like anxiety in viewing the function of the interpreter. They would ask us to consider music as a sort of aural sculpture, needing only to be displayed in order to convey to us the fullness of its power and its beauty, rather than as a being entranced, bound in cataleptic rigor save when some awakener breathes upon it and gives it momentary life.

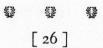

No doubt the feat needs explanation; but nothing is more certain than that we shall await that explanation long and vainly. The great interpreter and his feats are no more to be explained than is the artist whom we set in an unreal antithesis by calling him "creative." All great artists are "creative," whether they compose or perform or conduct, write or act; and creation is spun from the unknown and is compact of mystery.

What is music, as the lifeless notes exhibit it? An outline to be filled, indefiniteness to be defined, dust to be breathed upon, clay to be made flesh, inertness to be made flame, the sleep-bound to be awakened.

A melody has been defined as "a sequence of notes in which each has an intelligible value in relation to what came before or will come after." But only the interpreter of genius can make those values intelligible in the fullest sense.

If it were true that all one need do is to "let the music speak for itself," these instances of revelation, and others like them, would not await the advent of exceptional artists: they would spring as abundantly from the soil of music as dandelions on suburban lawns. Alas, we know that they do not. We know that apart from the lonely clan of rare interpreters there are ten thousand dull and commonplace executants filling the complacent ether and the auditoriums of the world with stillborn notes.

❦   ❦   ❦

The written notes are not the music: the music is the fluctuant reality behind the recorded symbols.

Since, therefore, there must be an interpreter, a middleman—even if it be only one's humble self, deciphering beneath one's study lamp the symbols that stand so incompletely and often misguidingly for the *Leonore No. 3,* or *Tristan,* or the E minor Symphony, or *La Mer*—the best we can do in the matter is to say whose account of Beethoven or Wagner or Brahms or Debussy we prefer to hear. Which means, in practice, that we must make choice as to the communicative personality that is to be interposed between ourselves and the composer.

If we elect that this spokesman shall be some well-disposed and admirably industrious routinier who fancies himself as, let us say, a conductor of Debussy, we shall find that what we are getting when we hear *La Mer* via that conductor is a travesty of the work: that it is Debussy condemned to utter the dull speech and to reflect the commonplace mind and imagination of a mediocrity.

If, on the other hand, we elect that this spokes-man shall be such an interpreter as Toscanini, we shall realize, if we be clear-minded and responsive, that music speaks to us completely only through a great imaginative spirit and an imperious will, brought in transforming contact with its material by an artist who thus becomes a creator in his own right. We shall find that the music has been sub-jected to the contact of an incandescent mind, and that we are hearing what we know, by some intui-tive capacity of recognition, to be the truth.

Thus music lives but intermittently—lives only when some quickening imagination, some flame of ardor and wonderment and belief, summons it to life.

It is this act of revivification that Toscanini has achieved in countless instances. It has always seemed enigmatic and unaccountable. It always will. To say that the process to which he subjects the music that he undertakes is baffling and inex-plicable is to understate the case. It is the most baf-fling of all phenomena, for it is nothing less than the ultimate mystery: the act of giving life to the

inanimate—an act both of generation and of resurrection.

❦ ❦ ❦

So we may recognize the great conductor, if we
are in doubt about the matter, by his magical power
of resuscitation. He has overheard

. . . the strange things said
By God to the bright hearts
Of those long dead . . .

He can live himself back into the imaginative world
of an alien century, can recover the beauty and significance that have sunk into the past, disclose the
hidden tie that binds it to our own disparate day,
re-creating, by a touch, something that Time had
almost taken for its own. He can give wings to
sloths, can quicken mummies, and lift the leaden
feet of the condemned. Like the spirit that is behind
the worlds, he covets the treasure of the humble.
He would prove to us that things which were conceived by men in their desire or their happiness or
their hope may sometimes be made to yield a mood
or an emotion or a loveliness altogether unsuspected
and astounding, if they be subjected to that wandlike
touch which can awake the sleepers and bring the
living closer to their fellows.

[30]

But above all, he reminds us that music at its greatest is not only what John Dewey called "essential experience," but that it gives meaning to the dark, fantastic confusions of existence. As we listen to a page of Beethoven or Bach or Brahms or Wagner, music divinely strong and harmonious and controlled, we remember that the artist's ultimate function is to impose an ideal pattern of lucidity and significance upon the meaningless disorder of the world. We realize that Beauty is man's sublime retort to the chaos and the savagery of life.

II

THE REAL HAYDN

O NE of Toscanini's major services in the cause
of musical truthtelling has been his disclosure
of Haydn's music in its true character.

For many years, Haydn as a symphonic composer was placed in a false light by the old and con-
ventional picture of him as essentially a lighthearted
classic in a periwig, who, oddly enough, was always
in good spirits. "His music," wrote an eminent historian, "was irradiated with the same geniality and
kindness as his character." This authority described
the music of Haydn as "cheerful and pleasant . . .
bringing a breeze of health from wholesome places."
Another eminent student of Haydn, Brenet, quoted
what Heine wrote of Monsigny, and applied it to
Haydn: "We find here the serenest grace, an ingenuous sweetness, a freshness like the perfume of

the woods, and poetry—but the poetry of perfect health."

One cannot listen to the average performance of Haydn without feeling that this traditional view of the man and his music governed the conception of the reading. Haydn the symphonist has for generations been regarded and performed as though he were merely genial and breezy and wholesome, ingenuous and fresh. He remains, for the average music lover and musician, "Papa Haydn," amiable, carefree, sturdy, and benignant. There are many who still think of him, with indulgent affection, as just a cheery, rather simple-minded fellow who has nothing very moving to say to a generation whose ears are filled with the music of the later Beethoven and Wagner and Schubert and Brahms and Debussy and Sibelius, or any of the other masters who speak a tonal language more satisfying to our spiritual needs.

Within recent years, however, the conviction has been growing upon critics and musicians that this standardized view of Haydn omits a good deal of the truth; they have begun to see that it is an unfortunate error and a gross injustice to think of Haydn's music as deficient in depth and sensibility.

The sunny-spirited and ingenuous "Papa

Haydn" of the familiar tradition is one side of that complete Haydn who is slowly emerging from the mists of tradition. Haydn was not always "genial": he was a master of poignant and affecting musical speech; one who taught Beethoven profounder truths than those of form.

He spoke often in his music with a depth and richness of feeling that the conventionalized legend stupidly denied him. If we need to be convinced of the reality of this greater Haydn, we have only to recall, among many similar examples, the remarkable Largo of the G major Symphony which was long familiar to music lovers as "No. 13" in the old numbering of Breitkopf and Härtel.[1] In this deeply felt movement, with its probing and meditative beauty, we recognize a precursor of the great slow movements of Beethoven's symphonies and quartets and sonatas. Here the older master anticipates the pupil who was to follow him, and gives us one of those interludes of self-communion, devout and noble, which we call "great" when we meet them in Haydn's successor, but not when we meet them in Haydn himself. And, if one seeks the fine and sensitive Haydn, examine the slow movement of the Symphony in B-flat major, the ninth of the London

[1] It is No. 88 in the Chronological List.

[34]

series, or the Adagio cantabile of the fourth of the London set, likewise in B-flat, with its harmonic subtlety and expressiveness.

❀   ❀   ❀

It is also to be noted that Haydn occasionally spoke the language of a time that followed his by more than half a century.

Return to that symphony of which I have spoken, the one in G major, No. 13 (88). When this symphony was written, the United States had not elected its first President. It was the year in which Philadelphia was stirred by the doings of the Constitutional Convention—the year in which for the first time (as John Adams remarked) "the thirteen clocks all struck together." In Europe, the French Revolution was still two years off; and the "Concerts Spirituels," for which this symphony of Haydn's was composed, attracted audiences of the highest distinction to the Salle des Gardes in the Tuileries, where the society known as the Concerts de la Loge Olympique held its meetings from 1786 until the year when the fall of the Bastille disturbed the ordered elegance of Parisian days and nights. Marie Antoinette was often seen there, with others

of the court, in full regalia. The orchestral players
fiddled and blew in satin knee breeches and embroid-
ered coats, and wore pretty shining swords, and the
lace on their cuffs often interfered with the bowing
of the violinists, unless they were especially deft.

It is true that Paris in those days liked to regard herself as preternaturally advanced: for had
she not witnessed the exploit of Franklin in "bringing down the thunder from the clouds"? Had she
not been present at the birth of mesmerism? Had
not Louis Claude de Saint-Martin published the
thrillingly esoteric reveries of *Le Philosophe in-
connu,* which everyone was reading and excitedly
discussing? And only two years before, Blanchard
had sailed through the air from Dover to Calais,
while de Villette, de Rozier, and d'Arlande had gone
heavenward in a fire balloon.

Yet the remorseless chronology of musical history tells us that this one of Haydn's Vallombrosan
symphonies is old. It was composed in 1787, and is
among the dozen which Haydn was commissioned
to write for the Concerts de la Loge Olympique.

This symphony is, therefore, one year older
than the three great ones of Mozart—the E flat, G
minor, and C major of 1788. Haydn himself was
fifty-five when he wrote it; his contemporary Mozart

was thirty-one; and the first performance of the first symphony of Beethoven was not to occur for thirteen years.

Yet so wayward and incalculable a thing is the musical imagination, that it is possible to find in this score, which is now more than a century and a half old, passages that are astonishing in their modernity, a modernity that, if it is scarcely Schönbergian, has at least a Wagnerian hue. Consider, for example, that charming passage in the first movement from which the face of Eva Pogner looks out with sweet archness, long before Wagner dreamed her into being in the linden-scented streets of Nuremberg; although in the symphony she has less of tremulous anxiety because of the brisker pace of Haydn's Allegro. But set this surprising passage beside Wagner's (composed some eighty years later), and note that Haydn's harmony is far more "modern" than Wagner's, which is not "modern" at all!

❧   ❧   ❧

No, Haydn is scarcely to be disposed of by thinking of him as the innocent prank-player of the *Surprise* Symphony, or the ingenuous Nature poet of *The Creation,* or as the abstract Historic Figure

[37]

whom the world has been inclined to patronize. Yet even so shrewd a critic as Berlioz could write nonsense about Haydn's music. "It belongs," he said, "to the kind of naïvely good and gay music that recalls the innocent joys of the fireside and the *pot-au-feu*. It goes and comes, never brusquely; . . . at nine o'clock it puts on a clean nightcap, says a prayer, and sleeps in the peace of the Lord."

Berlioz should have been ashamed of himself after he wrote that, for it is unforgivably misleading and unjust. The Haydn of the nightcap and the cheerful *pot-au-feu* existed, of course; but there is another and far more memorable Haydn—the thoughtful, sensitive, deep-throated Haydn; and Berlioz should not have overlooked him. For Haydn recalls what Mr. Paderewski observed of his native land at a certain session of the Council of the League of Nations. "Poland," he said, "may be too small for a great state, but she is much too great for a small state."

❀   ❀   ❀

In Toscanini's performances of all eighteenth century music—Vivaldi's, Haydn's, Mozart's—there are lessons for many conductors: lessons in how to refine without finicking, how to achieve nuance without affectation, how to mould a phrase without dislocating its jaw; lessons in the difference between an expressiveness that clogs and suffocates and an expressiveness that gives point and life; lessons in the adjustment of delicately opposed sonorities—as when, for example, in that delicious passage of the "Maggiore" section of the Andante in Haydn's *Clock* Symphony, where the first violins play C-natural against an upper C-sharp of the flute, Toscanini reminds us that a pianissimo for strings and a pianissimo for woodwind are not always birds of a feather.

But above all, there is, in addition to this exquisite calculation of lines and colors and sonorities, a suffusing vitality of conception that turns these utterances of another age into music of youthful power and a beauty that speaks to us as though it were contemporaneous and our own.

This service is especially valuable in the case of Haydn, whose music has so long been misconceived and undervalued. As Toscanini plays the greater slow movements of these symphonies, they sound with their proper breadth and gravity and amplitude of speech. Haydn the genial "classicist," Haydn the pious bourgeois of the foolish legend, disappears, and we find instead a grave and meditative poet, uttering nobly impassioned speech.

And who would have expected that Haydn, who in his finales is often made to seem cheerfully inconsequential, can be almost as electrifying as Beethoven in one of his sweepingly jocund moods?

We are made to realize, in short, that this music was composed not by a "classic" in a periwig, but by a man essentially contemporary with ourselves, actual in his passion, his tenderness, his melancholy, his humor, his virility.

No symphony of Haydn's is more familiar than the so-called "No. 13," in G major. Toscanini has often played it in America; and each time that he has done so he has given his hearers fresh cause for surprise. But we are not learning for the first time that his performances of even the most familiar music are an endlessly surprising series of rediscoveries.

It is possible that on each occasion when Toscanini confronts a score long known to himself, he finds that it presents new aspects to his inexhaustibly probing mind and imagination: for that is the way of the creative and the re-creative life—the way for him who gives, and for him who receives. A great

American said of friendship: "It is an exercise of the purest imagination and the rarest faith." And so it is with artists whose loftiness is measured by the degree of their humility.

III

BEETHOVEN

THE "EROICA"

For a huge majority of the music-loving public, Beethoven doubtless stands as music's sign and symbol. It was more than a century ago that an acute and liberal-minded Prince wrote to Beethoven that the effect of his music upon the public "defies explanation." "Posterity," he declared, "will render it homage, and will bless your memory." Oddly prophetic words!

The sensitive layman may not realize, as his professional brother does, how marvelous a tissue of ordered sound Beethoven has woven in his greater works; yet he knows very well what Beethoven means when he utters the grief of Everyman in the *Eroica* Symphony; or brings the loveliness of the created earth within the mind by a six-note phrase

[42]

of the violins in the *Pastoral;* or, in the Fifth, speaks to us superbly of "courage never to submit or yield, and what is else not to be overcome"; or, in the Ninth, shows us a vision of human love and generosity beyond the dreams of all but fools and saints and madmen. Experiencing such things, the responsive layman knows what music can be at its most assuaging, most releasing and exalting; and why it is that such music, in the hands of a creative master, may become the greatest of all imaginative expressions of the human spirit.

❀   ❀   ❀

In the hands of a master, yes; but not without the coöperation of a master interpreter: else the word that is spoken is unheard, or heard but incompletely.

Toscanini, in the course of his active and fruitful years among us, has made us aware that the creation and the re-creation of music are enigmatic things, and that the wisest course for musicians and critics to pursue is to be humble, undogmatic, and even inquiring about them; for there are two classes of persons for whom music remains a mystery:

the sentimental innocents who know it not at all, and the students who know it best.

Who can say why it is that there should be so slight a margin of difference between a musical phrase that is a mere transient commonplace and a phrase that will haunt the ears of men forever? "The artificer in ideas is the chief of workers," wrote Lord Dunsany: "for out of nothing he will make a piece of work that may stop a child from crying or lead nations to higher things." But whether he does this or not (if he be a composer) is often a mere matter of some intervallic or rhythmic constituent that you might suppose to be negligible. Change the D-sharp of the English horn and 'cellos, in the first chord of the *Tristan* Prelude, to D-natural, and you have a musical banality. Play it as Wagner wrote it, and you have inexplicable magic. Change the rhythm of the opening subject of the Allegretto of Beethoven's Seventh Symphony so that the two eighth-notes become a dotted-eighth and a sixteenth, and you have destroyed the beauty of the theme.

But the mystery that lies at the heart of all musical creation is no deeper than the mystery that baffles us when we are faced by such a phenomenon as the re-creative power of a great interpreter.

BEETHOVEN

It was said of Wagner as a conductor that he caused people to ask themselves in astonishment "how it was that this work, which they had long thought they knew, should suddenly have become a different thing?"

Those who have heard Toscanini's disclosures of great music must have felt in him a similar power and a like enigma. It is as if this artist knew the secret path to some miraculous Fountain of the Blind whose waters restore the eyes of the sightless: for sightless we are likely to become in the presence of accustomed pages over which we have bent so long that we no longer perceive what is actually there.

❀   ❀   ❀

It must be ranked among the major achievements of Toscanini since he came among us that he has made great music one of the most exciting things in the world. This is not because he has made it seem more exciting than it really is (for that is the way of the mere sensationalist), but because he has made it seem as great as it really is. In all aesthetic experience there is nothing so exciting as this—to realize, with the certainty that revelation always brings, that one is face to face with the full disclosure of a master's thought.

A realization of this kind is beyond argument and beyond doubt. Hearing the *Eroica* Symphony as Toscanini evokes it from his players, one knows that this is the *Eroica* as Beethoven had conceived it— not as it could ever have sounded from the wretched orchestras of his time, under their inadequate conductors; but the *Eroica* in its fulfilled reality, conforming to the ideal pattern which shaped its maker's thought.

Some such certain recognition of a thing consummately achieved, of a thing communicated in its fullness, must sweep over the minds of thousands among those who listen to this performance. Whenever Toscanini has conducted the *Eroica* before a visible audience, one has been aware of a curious and unusual note in its reception by the listeners: an answering of deep unto deep: the response that is always given by men's spirits to those who could truthfully say to them, less in pride than in humility, "I speak not fictitious things, but that which is certain and most true."

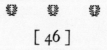

There are some who would rank this symphony first among the Nine; and it is occasionally said that Beethoven himself shared this preference. The incident on which that assertion has been based occurred one evening at Nussdorf in the summer of 1817, when Beethoven and the poet Kuffner were enjoying a fish supper together at the tavern "Zur Rose." There was a full moon, and Beethoven and his companion sat till midnight on the terrace, with the rushing brook and the swollen Danube before them. "Tell me frankly," asked Kuffner, "which is your favorite among your symphonies?"

Luckily for Kuffner, the unpredictable Ludwig was in good humor, and he answered, amiably and without hesitation, "the *Eroica*."

Kuffner seems to have been astonished, for he remarked, "I should have guessed the C minor."

"No," insisted Beethoven: "the *Eroica*."

But it is important to remember that this incident occurred in the year 1817, when Beethoven had completed only eight of his symphonies. The incomparable Ninth was not finished until seven years later.

If Beethoven had been asked the same question in 1824 that Kuffner asked him in 1817, would he have given the same answer? If only we knew! We do know this, however: that Carl Czerny, the pianist and pedagogue who was a pupil and favorite of Beethoven, used to relate as a fact that some time after the first performance of the Ninth Symphony, Beethoven said to a circle of his intimate friends that he regarded the Choral Finale of the Ninth as a "mistake," and that he intended to discard it and write an instrumental finale in its stead—an idea which he had entertained years before, but had abandoned. Perhaps Czerny was romancing; or perhaps his memory played him false—for he told this story a quarter of a century after Beethoven's death. Happily, Beethoven did not discard the Choral Finale of the Ninth Symphony, though he had plenty of time in which to do so—he lived for almost three years after the first performance of the work.

So, in this matter, we can only speculate, and cling to Kuffner's assertion that Beethoven preferred the *Eroica* Symphony at least to any of the other forerunners of the Ninth.

Fortunately, we do not need to choose among the uncompanioned Nine—we have them all, and can turn from one to the other as they are set before us, with their different expressions of the moods and visions and aspirations of a great nature, their different outlooks upon the world and the heavens and the mystery and sublimity of the soul of man.

❧   ❧   ❧

The *Eroica* brings us, for the first time in music, to the high places of the symphonic world. And here, for the first time in the progress of the symphonies, we find Beethoven dealing with great issues. Here, specifically, we meet with that unprecedented Beethoven whom we recognize, in Wagner's phrase, as "a Titan wrestling with the gods." This is the heroic and defiant Beethoven of the *Eroica's* first movement, subduing us by his immensity of passion, his noble severity and directness. The second movement, the Funeral March, with its overpowering blend of grandeur and poignancy, is the dark glory of the *Eroica*. Is it not to be ranked, together with the Crucifixus from Bach's B minor Mass and Wagner's Funeral Hymn for Siegfried, among the unapproachable trio of music's supreme laments? In the third movement, we encounter— again for the first time in the symphonies—one of those unparalleled scherzos, of which only Beethoven knew the liberating word, that sweep through his music, jocund and tumultuous, like the sport of

[49]

some timeless elemental spirit at play among the comets and the worlds. The fourth movement, based on a theme which Beethoven had already used in his *Prometheus,* is employed in the *Eroica* Finale as the subject of a series of variations; and it is easy to agree with those who see in this magnificent Finale, with its profusion of ideas, a symbolization of the power of the mind in action, as though Beethoven had meant to glorify the exercise of man's creative will as the triumphant justification of our human living.

The magnitude of the *Eroica* is commensurate with its greatness of substance. Throughout its vast extent the score remains a thing of ageless wonder, with a detachment from period and manner that stamps the surpassing masterwork. Nothing in it sounds outworn. And who else could have introduced a double fugue [1] into a funeral march, and charged the formalism of the old device with such an intensity of tragic grief—who, indeed, but Beethoven, with his boundless humanity and compassion? For the composer of this symphony is not only towering and heroic, he is also deeply pitiful and intimate and very human. Some of us, as we listen

[1] This "solemn double fugue," as Tovey calls it, evoked from Felix Weingartner the fortunate epithet, "Aeschylean."

to the closing pages of the Dirge, in which the music speaks with so fathomless a tenderness of human loss and suffering, may remember what Mendelssohn tells us of the Baroness von Ertmann and her experience with Beethoven. "She related," says Mendelssohn, "that when she lost her last child, Beethoven at first did not want to come into the house; at length he invited her to visit him, and when she came, he sat himself down at the piano, and said simply: 'We will now talk to each other in tones'; and for over an hour he played without stopping, and, as she remarked, 'he told me everything, and at last brought me comfort.' "

❦   ❦   ❦

Like all great works of art, Beethoven's *Eroica* is boundless, not to be encompassed. We may view it, as we think, from every possible standpoint; we may discuss it endlessly in its aspects as "absolute" music, or as program music, or as an expression of Beethoven's relation to his time and to the strutting Lilliputian whom he had supposed to be a hero; and still we shall not have begun to do more than touch the music's surfaces, tentatively, with hesitant, groping fingers, like a blind man trying to inform himself

concerning the shape and substance of some unknown object that extends beyond his reach and
estimation.

No one knows exactly what Beethoven meant
to say in the *Eroica*. Apparently [2] its inspiration was
an idealized image of Napoleon Bonaparte that existed in Beethoven's mind before he heard the news
that the First Consul had proclaimed himself Em-
peror. As Ries told the story, Beethoven, learning
that his idol was only an ordinary mortal after all,
expunged from the score of the symphony, in a burst
of disillusioned rage, the inscription that had referred to Bonaparte, exclaiming bitterly: "Now we
shall see him trample on the rights of men to gratify
his own ambitions; he will exalt himself above
everyone, and become a tyrant!" When Beethoven
published the symphony two years later, the name
of the "hero" who had betrayed his faith did not
appear on the score; but there was a tragically
pathetic, tragically ironic reference to him in the
title, which ran: "Heroic Symphony, Composed to
Celebrate the Memory of a Great Man."

[2] The traditions, descended from Czerny and other friends
of Beethoven, that the opening Allegro is a description of a naval
battle, and that the Dirge commemorates the death of Nelson or
General Abercrombie, are dismissed by Thayer as "mistakes"—
though the late Paul Bekker, in his careful study of Beethoven,
gives credence to the tradition concerning Abercrombie.

BEETHOVEN

The sense of that betrayal died with Beethoven. It is survived by a reality that cannot die. The Bonaparte of whom Beethoven had dreamed did not exist in time or space or history. But the sublimated image that had been imprinted upon the mind of Beethoven endures unchangeably, secure from mutilation or destruction. It lives for us in the *Eroica* Symphony, as it lived in the composer's thoughts before his hero failed him. Beethoven had conceived of Bonaparte as a symbol of human emancipation, a flaming torch thrust in the face of tyranny and wrong. He had lived in the firm belief, as Schindler informs us, that Bonaparte would "make a beginning for the general happiness of mankind." Beethoven saw in his idol the promise of a new age, the embodied spirit of a world reborn. Perhaps, in his exaltation, he remembered that sublime passage from *The Bacchae* of Euripides—

> To stand from fear set free,
> To breathe and wait;
> To hold a hand uplifted over Hate . . .

All of Beethoven's sorrowful tenderness at the thought of human agony, all his compassionate indignation at the wrongs that might at last be righted by the incorruptible hero of his visions—all this, in

[53]

its undying essence, went into the music of the
Eroica Symphony, and lives there for us unalter-
ably, immune from the accidents of human weak-
ness and treachery and defeat.

❦　　❦　　❦

Yet most of the eminent commentators of the
last century or so who discussed the *Eroica* were
not content to tell us that Beethoven in this symphony is disclosing a lofty concept of human living,
an image of spiritual experience. Instead, they tried
to find in the music specific pictures, incidents,
dramas, events. It is scarcely surprising that this
way of viewing Beethoven's symphony should have
led them into endless and unnecessary difficulties.

They imposed upon the work a bewildering
variety of interpretations. They found no difficulty
in explaining the first and second movements, in
which they chose to discover musical delineations of
the life and death of a hero: for the first movement is full of heroic struggle, and the second is
avowedly a Funeral March. But endless trouble was
caused by the inconvenient fact that the Scherzo
comes after the Funeral March, instead of before.
And they were puzzled by the Finale in variation

[54]

form. The commentators labored to extricate themselves from a predicament into which they would never have fallen, as one of them observed, "if only Beethoven had been considerate enough to make his Scherzo precede his slow movement, instead of following it. Then the progress of the hero would have been detected plainly enough in the four movements: his aspirations and struggles in the first, his recreations in the second, his death in the third, and his glorification in the last."

As it is, let us see what some of the commentators have found it necessary to do: Marx's scheme for the work might be outlined as follows: "First movement:—an ideal battle, as the purport of a heroic life. Second movement—a midnight inspection of the battle-field. Third movement—merrymaking in camp. Fourth movement—celebration of peace. Lenz's conception imagined the first movement as portraying the life and death of the hero, the second movement as a lament for his death, the third as a truce at the grave, and the fourth as a funeral feast and heroic song of praise. Another commentator likened the Scherzo to an armistice which the soldiers devote to pleasures. "Some seize their rifles and hurry into the woods, and we hear the merry fanfares of their hunting horns." Still another commentator pictured the variations of the Finale as "following one upon the other like a procession of many generations of men marching up to the cyclopean monument erected to the hero, and crowning it with wreaths and flowers."

Attempted explanations of this literal kind are superfluous and irrelevant. It is not for any one of us to say that he knows what Beethoven wished us to hear in the *Eroica*. I venture to believe that we shall come closer to the meaning of the work if we think of it as music which is not concerned with actual and specific things, with incidents and pictures and events, but with an ideal imaginative pattern of truth and feeling and aspiration.

A student of the history of musical expression has remarked that in certain of the Italian madrigals of the late sixteenth century the composers have chosen to set music to poems which have no profound significance; yet the music composed for them seems charged with an intensity and depth of meaning that almost overwhelm the words. When we ponder the reason for this, it becomes evident that words such as "death," "pain," "care," occurring in poems that are not especially poignant, were treated by the composer in their full and essential meaning, regardless of their context. Thus a poem of formal and stereotyped character, concerned, perhaps, with the woes of a rejected lover, would serve as a framework over which the composer would weave a musical tapestry embodying his whole conception of the tragedy of human grief and the finality of death.

Music, at its greatest, has always been able to do this, finding its way to regions where words or actualities cannot follow it. I believe that Beethoven, dreaming of a Bonaparte who never lived, composed in the *Eroica* Symphony music that has nothing essentially to do with history, but with heroism and humanity—music that projects a vision of the tragic and heroic destiny of man.

But whatever "program" we do or do not attach to the *Eroica,* the music itself remains for men to marvel at. We shall find, in the Symphony as a whole, not Beethoven the seer, the prophet, the mystic—Beethoven of the fathomless gaze: *that* Beethoven is to be sought rather in the last sonatas and quartets, in the *Missa Solemnis,* in parts of the Ninth Symphony. But the Beethoven who could bestride the world and shoulder the heavens and affright the winds, a figure half granite and half flame; a Titan who laments and laughs and exults with a hugeness more than human: this Beethoven, heartbreaking and terrible and jocose, speaks from the *Eroica* Symphony.

❧   ❧   ❧

For every phase of the *Eroica,* Toscanini discovers the releasing interpretative word. His deeds of illuminative penetration, of inspired justice, are as nearly fabulous as the technical mastery that orders and controls them.

He knows how to fill an imaginative design of flawless symmetry and beauty with a tide of life and energy so potent that one would expect it to overflow its limits, become unmanageable and chaotic. But the governing will is never relaxed; the sobriety, the impeccable taste, the inner serenity of this artist, who is both bountiful and austere, control the storm and master the winds and tides of his imaginative fury; so that he can unloose the tremendous passions of the first movement of the *Eroica* without congesting the surface of the music or distorting the beauty of its line. That dire passage of the Development section in which Beethoven seems to hurl his rage and defiance and despair against a heedless sky is conveyed to us with a Mediterranean clarity and a Gothic immensity and power.

What Toscanini accomplishes in his divulging of this symphony is in essence a repetition of what he achieves with other music of comparable magnitude. Quite simply, with the blended humility and imperiousness of the cardinal interpreter, he comes into the presence of these moods and imaginings of Beethoven: pours out upon them his own responsive fineness, his own flame and sensibility, his own richness of living and experience, and gives us the astonishing and matchless product.

He knows, for example, how to imbue with the last extremity of dolorous significance that A-flat of the first violins which sounds as a kind of piteous exhalation in the fragment of the main theme that follows the fugue in the Dirge. Yet this isolated note has a delicate inevitability in its structural relation to the whole enormous fabric that only a consummate master of design would have known how to give it. For these minutiae do not obtrude; the vast pattern of the score still moves gigantically across the tonal skies: we hear the cyclopean tread of Beethoven's mighty music, with its appalling immensity of grief and terror, and its climax on that unexampled page in which the implacably reiterated octaves of the brass cut menacingly through the orchestral gloom, as if Beethoven had for a moment opened some Seventh Seal of an ancestral revelation, and the trumpets of the Apocalypse had begun to sound, and the sun and stars had fallen into the abyss.

❧   ❧   ❧

There is in every masterpiece what a poet has called an "infinite patience of beauty." It awaits us always, deeply resigned and unperturbed, until we are ready to have it speak to us. It awaits, longest, the elect interpreter; but when he has come, and the consummation is achieved, there is little that we who are merely witnesses can find to say.

THE FIFTH AND THE "PASTORAL"

It is the natural assumption of music lovers that the Beethoven symphony which we know as the "Sixth" (the *Pastoral*) was completed after the so-called "Fifth," the C minor. But, as a matter of fact, the chronological relation of these two symphonies to each other has not yet been ascertained. Clio, when we press her too closely on this point, drops her veil over her face, puts her fingers delicately in her ears, and turns away. She declines to tell us whether, for example, the C minor Symphony was completed in

1807 or in 1808 (Thayer, in his definitive Life of Beethoven, gives both dates).

According to the eminent Beethoven scholar, Nottebohm, Beethoven sketched both the *Pastoral* and the C minor symphonies, in part, during the same period. Nottebohm concluded, from a study of Beethoven's sketchbooks, that the C minor was completed in March, 1808, and the *Pastoral* later— though there is a remote possibility that the *Pastoral,* which was written down with unusual speed, was finished as soon as the C minor. Thayer calls attention to the circumstance that "at the Vienna concert of December 22, 1808, when both symphonies were produced, the *Pastoral,* which we now know as 'No. 6,' was numbered 5, and the C minor, now known as 'No. 5,' was numbered 6."

For many years the *Pastoral* Symphony took precedence over the C minor in the numbering of Beethoven's symphonies, the *Pastoral* being called the "Fifth" and the C minor the "Sixth" on concert programs as late as 1820. Both symphonies were published (in parts) in 1809, the C minor in April, the *Pastoral* in May.

Johann Friedrich Reichardt has told us that Vienna concert of December 22, 1808, lasted four hours—from 6:30 till 10:30. "I accepted with hearty thanks the kind offer of Prince Lobkowitz to let me sit in his box," says Reichardt. "There we endured the bitterest cold, and realized that it is easy to get too much of a good thing, and still more of a loud thing . . ." The unhappy Reichardt and his princely host were unable to escape: "For the box was in the first balcony near the stage, so that the orchestra and Beethoven conducting it were near at hand; and many a failure in the performance vexed our patience in the highest degree. . . . It had been impossible to get a single full rehearsal."

Reichardt discussed the two new symphonies. Of the *Pastoral,* he remarked that "each movement was very long, complete, and developed, full of lively painting and brilliant thoughts and figures; and this, a pastoral symphony, lasted much longer than a whole court concert lasts in Berlin."

The C minor he described as "a great, highly developed, too long symphony. A gentleman next us assured us he had noticed at rehearsal that the violoncello part alone—and the violoncellists were kept very busy—covered thirty-four pages. It is true that the copyists here understand how to spread out their copy, as the law scriveners do at home."

In our time, the C minor Symphony seems anything but "too long." Especially as Toscanini plays it, the work seems concentrated and close-knit beyond almost any other of the Nine.

Years ago, when he first played it here, there were some who declared amusingly that this account of Beethoven was "insufficiently Teutonic." Whether Toscanini's conception is sufficiently or insufficiently "Teutonic" seems to me beside the point. I am certain that it is heroic and beautiful, and as great in its tensity and sweep of drama as the symphony itself : tremendous when Beethoven is tremendous; electric, incisive, swift, in those passages where the music drives like a flaming sword; inscrutable and overwhelming, as in the passage of transition that leads from the tenebrous, suspensive mystery of the Scherzo into the dazzling noon of the Finale, with its huge blaze and burst of golden, epic sound, its communicated sense of a mastering spirit sovereign above the battle and the worlds.

❦   ❦   ❦

That unslaked romanticist, Sir George Grove, was persuaded that Beethoven, in this most famous of all symphonies, concealed an intimate and troubled chapter of his turbulent career. Sir George, in his widely read book on the Beethoven Symphonies,

[63]

believed that the C minor gives us musical portraits of Beethoven himself and of the Countess Therese von Brunswick—whom Sir George does not hesitate to identify as the original of Beethoven's so-called "Immortal Beloved," the mysterious woman to whom Beethoven wrote the impassioned love-letters that all the world has read.

Sir George Grove was a conscientious student of Beethoven's life and art, and a devoted admirer of his genius. We are all under a large debt of gratitude to him for his fidelity and eloquence. But some of us do not find it easy to share his beliefs concerning the nature of the ideas and emotions that found expression in the Fifth Symphony. When Sir George identified the Countess Therese von Brunswick as Beethoven's "Immortal Beloved," and told us that we may find a portrait of her in the Fifth Symphony, he was, with the best will in the world, offering us mere conjectures.

It is necessary to remember that the original of Beethoven's "Immortal Beloved" is still unknown. A century of research by musical scholars has left us with no more certain knowledge about that fascinating enigma than we had before. Perhaps we shall never know who she was; there are at least half a dozen candidates for the honor of having inspired Beethoven's impassioned and tragic letters, and we are all at liberty to examine the evidence and make our own choice.

❦   ❦   ❦

We shall find ourselves on much firmer ground if we consider the Fifth Symphony not as the expression of a specific experience, but rather of certain spiritual and emotional states which made the experience possible. In other words, it seems likely that this music tells us more concerning Beethoven's way of thinking and feeling about life than it does about any facts of his existence. But so intensely did Beethoven visualize these conceptions and feelings, that they become for us, in his music, far more real than any tonal portraits of human beings could ever be.

In one of the most searching examinations of Beethoven's mind and art that have been written, the late J. W. N. Sullivan's admirable book on the master, this characteristic of Beethoven's music is tellingly set forth. Mr. Sullivan reminds us that certain aspects of life had such immense importance for Beethoven that they became, in a sense, personified. Thus he seems, at one period of his creative

[65]

life, to have had a personified idea of Fate, which was his name for those things in life that call forth the heroic in man. A conviction of the need and importance of the heroic principle persisted in his mind. As he grew older, he came to view this contest as one between two inner principles: assertion and submission; and the entire conflict was transferred to the inner stage of his mind and imagination.

※　　※　　※

In his later years, he was to express a view of Destiny less obviously dramatic and exciting, though far more shattering and terrific. In the Ninth Symphony we shall meet this appalling conception of Fate as a mere blind and purposeless and destructive force, as aimless as a lightning-bolt; and Beethoven's final utterances as a composer tell us of the various ways in which the human spirit may deal with the implacable and hideous thing—by acquiescence, by resignation, by transcendence. Yet the basic impulse never ceased to be heroic, whether, like faith, it moved the mountains of the spirit's world, or whether it shaped some mystical inner vision.

But in the Fifth Symphony, the beginnings of which appear to date from Beethoven's early thirties, when he was mustering all his enormous courage to deal with the onset of his deafness, he was still objectifying Fate as an enemy, not merely as an impersonal force. And what we know of his development as an artist justifies us in viewing the Fifth Symphony as a window into the mind and imagination which conceived this encounter between a heroic spirit and that apparently malignant power menacing our happiness and our peace. In the symphony, this struggle begins at once with the shock and challenge of the opening bars. It interrupts the delusive serenity of the slow movement; it is recalled by the defiant energy and the mysterious suspense of the Scherzo; and it is ended by the spiritual triumph of which we learn from the Finale.

❁   ❁   ❁

It would be interesting to know more than we do concerning the reaction of the public of 1808 to the two symphonies that were produced on December 22nd of that year at Vienna, the Fifth and the *Pastoral*. Did the *Pastoral* suffer then, as it does today—in the estimation of certain unreasonable observers—by comparison with the C minor?

When otherwise responsible commentators see

fit to describe the Sixth Symphony as "a dreadful decline and fall from the Fifth," one cannot but ask just what it is that they expect of it. Obviously, the *Pastoral* Symphony is not a tremendous utterance like the C minor or the *Eroica*. But there is far more in the *Pastoral* than Beethoven's own too-modest definition of its purpose would lead us to expect. It is not a mere "recollection of country life." On another occasion, Beethoven spoke more justly of his symphony. "When you wander through the mysterious forests of pine," he wrote to a friend at Baden nine years after he had composed the work, "remember that Beethoven often made poetry there." That gives us something of the spirit that is reflected in Schindler's account of the walk that he and Beethoven took together on a certain sunny day toward the end of Beethoven's life:

"After visiting the bath-house at Heiligenstadt and the adjoining garden," wrote Schindler, "and talking over many a pleasant reminiscence having reference to his creations, we continued our walk toward the Kahlenberg in the direction of Grinzing [*sic*].[3] Strolling through the delightful meadow

[3] Schindler's memory seems to have been at fault here. The "walk toward the Kahlenberg," it has been pointed out, took the strollers northward into the valley between Heiligenstadt and

valley between Heiligenstadt and the latter village, which was crossed by a gently murmuring brook that hurries down from a neighboring mountain and is bordered by high elms, Beethoven stopped repeatedly and let his glance, full of blissful feeling, wander over the beautiful landscape. Then, seating himself upon the grass and leaning against an elm, he asked me whether there was no yellow-hammer to be heard in the tops of those trees. But all was still. He then said, 'Here I composed the *Scene by the Brook,* and the yellow-hammer up there, the quails, nightingales, and cuckoos round about, composed with me.' "

We get, there, a hint of the Nature lover who is discoverable behind the leafy curtains of the *Pastoral.*

To Beethoven's devout and passionate spirit, the "Return to Nature" was an action as spontaneous and naïve and profound as the inclination of the medieval mystic's soul toward God. Beethoven believed that wisdom broods upon the hills and in the long forest aisles; that sustenance for the heart could be garnered from sunlight and free winds, and spiritual peace drunk from quiet valleys as from a

Nussdorf, where a bust of the composer now marks that "Scene by the Brook" that Beethoven immortalized in his symphony.

divinely proffered cup. He would have understood
that ecstatically confident cry of a Celtic dreamer of
today: "Death will never find us in the heart of the
wood!" To his mind had come the thought that
illumination of an unequalled kind was yielded by
"the mere common green of the world." For Beethoven, there were confirmations and reinforcements
in that murmuring and timeless mystery that engrossed the meditations of a later poet: "the mystery
that seeks expression in this universal green—the
mystery of that which multiplies, forever issuing
out of that which multiplies not. Or is the seeming
lifeless itself life—only a life more silent still, more
hidden?"

Beethoven copied from his beloved and much-
thumbed volume of Sturm's *Lehr und Erbauungs-
Buch* this passage: "One might rightly denominate
Nature the school of the heart; she clearly shows us
our duties towards God and our neighbor. Hence, I
wish to become a disciple of this school and to offer
Him my heart. Desirous of instruction, I would seek
after that wisdom which no disillusionment can
confute; I would gain a knowledge of God, and
through this knowledge I shall obtain a foretaste of
celestial felicity." Beethoven himself wrote to the
Baroness von Drosdick that he was convinced of the

fact that "no one loves country life as I do. It is as if every tree and every bush could understand my mute enquiries and respond to them." Some years after he had completed the *Pastoral,* and while he was finishing the Seventh Symphony, he exclaimed: "Almighty God, in the woods I am blessed. Happy everyone in the woods! Every tree speaks through Thee. O God! What glory in the woodland! On the heights is peace—peace to serve Him." Sir George Grove records a tradition that Beethoven refused to take possession of an engaged lodging because there were no trees near the house.

"How is this? Where are your trees?"

"We have none."

"Then the house won't do for me. I love a tree more than a man."

Charles Neate, the British musician who knew Beethoven, told Thayer, the master's biographer, that Nature was "his [Beethoven's] nourishment."

❋   ❋   ❋

To the music of the *Pastoral* Symphony Beethoven transferred his delight in the beauty of the world. Back of its simple and ingenuous picturing of rural scenes and incidents and adventures—its brookside reveries, its merrymaking and thunderstorms and shepherds' hymns—is something more than their mere emotional equivalents, something rarer, less accessible, than that "expression of feeling" by which the composer thought to justify his "portraiture": back of these evident aspects rises the image of a poet and believer transfixed by the immortal spectacle, and recording his awe and tenderness in songs that cannot help being canticles of praise. It is easy to suppose that Beethoven might have been the original of that ancient legend told by a man of the North to a poet of the North: "A monk wandered into the fields, and a lark began to sing. The monk had never heard a lark before, and he stood there entranced, until the bird and its song had become part of the heavens. Then he went back to the monastery and found there a doorkeeper whom he did not know and who did not know him. He told them his name, but that was no help. Finally they looked through the books of the monastery, and these revealed that there had been one of his name there a hundred or more years before. Time had been blotted out while he listened to the lark."

As you listen to the music of this symphony, with its reverence and fervor and sweet gravity, you may remember also the folk tale of the old man who could always be found at sunrise looking seaward through the shadow of the woods, with his white locks blowing in the wind that rose out of the dawn, and who, being asked why he was not at his prayers, replied: "Every morning like this I take off my hat to the beauty of the world."

❀   ❀   ❀

Beethoven could do wondrous things with that great voice of his. He could address us overwhelmingly as a prophet, as a revealer of mysteries: he could sing with the morning stars in their exalted hours. But was he ever more persuasive, more intimately touching, more tenderly to be cherished, than as a tonal celebrant of the natural world? Some of us, thinking of the *Pastoral* Symphony, are fain to doubt it. Was ever Beethoven's creative imagination more cleansed and purified than it is in this enamoring and bountiful work?

It is true that Nature, in this music, is seldom touched with the kind of magic that the Romanticists and the Neo-Romanticists, from Weber to Debussy, have brought to their evocations of the outer world. Nor shall we hear, in the music of the *Pastoral,* the hushed and otherworldly rumor of "evenings full of

the linnet's wings," the sound of "bee-loud glades."
But it may be that this music holds for us rewards
more deep and lasting. It is the very sign and symbol
of divine simplicity and candor, a reverent hymn of
adoration in praise of the loveliness and sublimity
of the created earth. It is Beethoven's testament of
his response to the holiness of the natural world.
Beneath the fresh and limpid loveliness of this
music, beneath its quiet tenderness, its humor and
jollity and drama, are an infinite purity and innocence, an unplumbed and fathomless wisdom of the
heart. Beethoven the seer and prophet of the mystical quartets and the great Mass, Beethoven the
seraphic singer of the Ninth's Adagio, the sky-
shouldering rhapsodist of its Choral Finale, is here
ingenuous and devout and blithe. But there is something else in this music, if we are prepared to seek
and find it: these musical meditations, so naïve and
so profound, are the product of an imagination like
unto that of another lover of the created earth to
whom the wind was brother and the grass sister.
The music tells us of things that are "newly made,
and awaiting new names," things worshipped with a
disembodied passion.

🌼 🌼 🌼

What Toscanini accomplishes in his playing of the *Pastoral* Symphony has long been, for some of us, his most endearing achievement. He becomes, in setting it before us, Beethoven's other self, sharing Beethoven's directness of approach and Beethoven's intimacy of relationship with that natural world which he adored unspeakably.

When Toscanini plays the work there cannot be many who need to be assured that this symphony is among the rarest that any composer has vouchsafed us: music that has caught up into itself all of that which Thoreau called "the indescribable innocence and beneficence of Nature"—of sun and wind and rain, of Summer and Autumn, of the bounty and everlastingness of soil and sky, and the savor of those who live closely and intimately with recurrent things.

It is reassuring to hear this symphony played with such fullness of belief and such plenary devotion as Toscanini brings to it. Nothing could exceed the affection and the care that this indefatigable master lavishes upon every moment of the score. The choicest of its pages—which I take leave to think are those of the first movement, wherein the tone-poet looks about his beloved countryside, murmuring delightedly, perhaps, his favorite line, "The

TOSCANINI AND GREAT MUSIC

morning air has gold to spare," or farewelling the decrescent sun in the environs of Mödling—these pages are re-created by Toscanini with inimitable justness and delicacy of perception.

The beautiful opening melody of the first violins at the beginning of the second movement, the "Scene by the Brook," which so often from other hands is merely sweet and viscous, like spilt syrup on a tablecloth, issues from Beethoven's freed imagination, released and fluent, with the tempo faithfully as Beethoven marked it. Later, the nightingale that warbles so oddly like a flute, the quail disguised as an accomplished oboist, the cuckoo hidden in a B-flat clarinet—these sound for us with all their old and fragrant charm, their playful humor extraordinarily enhanced; and the meditative song of the violins that turns the jest to poetry is exquisitely adjusted to the imaginative key of the episode, hackneyed in its usual effect, but new and delectable under the hands of its rekindling interpreter.

❀   ❀   ❀

This music will always and perpetually renew itself so long as there are poets to understand it, to feel again and to recover its beauty and gravity and devoutness, with the insight and the vivifying power that Toscanini brings to it. With what poetry and tenderness he captures the mood and the image of Beethoven's quiet brook in those delicious phrases that should sing and flow as the brook sang and flowed through Beethoven's quickened fancy! How communicative is the fervor of the hymn of praise in the Finale, so that we know at once, as Beethoven knew, what kind of roof the heavens extended over these shepherds and these peasants, "what seasons ministered to them, what winds were their breath," and what serenity they borrowed from the fields and woods and hills!

In conducting this symphony, Toscanini is sharing a creative experience, living at the music's source. Thus Beethoven could have said to him, in Pascal's words, "You would not have sought me if you had not already found me."

THE SEVENTH

It is a century and a quarter since Beethoven's Seventh Symphony was first heard by the astonished ears of men—for, like other surprising expressions of genius, this symphony was not received with unanimous approval. The public seems to have been enthusiastic, for Spohr, who played among the violins in the orchestra, tells us that the symphony gave "extraordinary pleasure," and that the second movement, the Allegretto, was repeated. But Weber, Beethoven's great contemporary, was deeply disturbed by the music—he thought that a certain passage in the first movement proved that Beethoven was "ripe for the madhouse."

The Seventh Symphony was first performed at a benefit concert in the large hall of the University in Vienna, December 8, 1813. The concert had aroused unusual public interest in Vienna, and everyone was eager to help. Beethoven, though he was then very deaf, conducted the performance of his symphony—probably not to its advantage. Sir George Grove reminds us that there was a black-haired, sallow, thickset, spectacled lad of fifteen in Vienna at that time, named Franz Schubert, son of a parish schoolmaster in the suburbs, who had completed his first symphony only six weeks before; and it is probable that he was somewhere in the audience.

The orchestral performance, says Spohr, was "quite masterly," though Beethoven's contribution to its effect must have been negligible. Spohr's account, in his autobiography, has often been quoted, but it is so vivid and remarkable as a thumbnail sketch of Beethoven in his occasional function as conductor that it bears repeating. "At this concert," says Spohr, "I first saw Beethoven conduct. Often as I had heard of his conducting, it surprised me extremely. He was accustomed to convey the marks of expression to the band by the most peculiar motions of his body. Thus, at a *sforzando,* he tore his arms, which were before crossed on his breast, violently apart. At a soft passage he crouched down, bending lower the softer the tone. At a *crescendo* he raised himself by degrees, until, at the climax, he sprang up to his full height; and without knowing it, he would often at the same time shout aloud."

That must have been a strange spectacle, indeed —the agonized contortions of Beethoven the conductor, grotesque and almost ludicrous, applied to the rhythmical poetry of Beethoven the composer, with its measured beauty and its magical grace!

❦ ❦ ❦

It would be rash to attempt a guess at the number of times the Seventh Symphony has been performed in America since it was introduced here not far from a century ago—on November 18, 1843.

Yet it is not too much to say that those of us who love this work, with its quenchless gusto and vitality, its passion of rhythmic life, can never feel that we have heard it too often, or that we have even begun to exhaust the power and the fascination that it exerts—this music that seems to speak to us in Ariel's jocund words:

> I drink the air before me, and return
> Or ere your pulse twice beat.

It is likely that many of us, hearing this symphony and other works of comparable inspiration and familiarity, have reminded ourselves that the disclosure of unsuspected treasures of beauty and significance in an intimately known masterpiece remains the most memorable form of aesthetic revelation. These disclosures may come about through the special genius of such an interpreter as Toscanini, or through some mysterious quickening in our own minds and imaginations. But however they come, the result is the same: some veil is lifted, and a moment of sudden light floods and illuminates the countenance that we thought we knew so well. Those who have listened to Toscanini's restitution of that which belongs of right to the Beethoven of the Seventh Symphony, or those who possess the superlative recording that he made of it in 1936, will know what he has accomplished for this music. Never, in my own experience, has the score achieved so lucid and full a realization—especially (if one would pick and choose) in the lyric turbulence of that unparalleled Finale, that "Dionysian orgy" (as Wagner called it) of rhythmic ecstasy and superhuman grace. Even the frenzy that takes possession of this music does not distract the attention of the leader and his players from significant details that many performances ignore—as, for example, the exactness of the phrasing in the opening theme of the movement, as Beethoven releases the flight of those elemental songs and rhythms that course through his music like the winds and gales of some pristine and magically recovered Spring.

❀　　❀　　❀

The greatest music always thus renews itself for us, always manifests this quality of changefulness. Music thus stamped—whether it is by Beethoven or Bach or Haydn, Brahms or Wagner, or some other master equally vital and inexhaustible—may, indeed, be recognized by this simple test: that it seems to mean different things to different genera-

[81]

tions—that it speaks to succeeding epochs in varying ways. It may even change its aspect and dimen-
sions for us as individuals, extending and deepen-
ing itself in unaccountable ways. Few of us have
failed to notice that a given music that wore for us
one face in years gone by, may wear a different one
today. Music that has been breathed upon by a creative spirit is not eternally set and changeless. It is
an unstable and fluctuating thing, infinitely mysterious, disclosing new surfaces and unsuspected
depths to ears that had accustomed themselves to
its dear familiarities.

❦　　❦　　❦

Beethoven's Seventh Symphony is a case in
point. Think, for example, of the many and con-
flicting things that this music has meant for its interpreters! Scarcely any other musical work has
been so variously and so remorselessly interpreted.
Who has not taken a hand at the task of telling us
what this music "means"? From Berlioz to Isadora
Duncan, from Alberti to Schumann, a vast and innumerable multitude of commentators, expounders,
interpreters, have lavished upon it their fancy and

their eloquence. And what has not been read into
this symphony?

We are all familiar with Wagner's belief that
the Seventh Symphony represents an exalted expression of the dance in its highest condition, "the
happiest realization of the movements of the body
in its ideal form"—a view of Beethoven's music
which has been taken perhaps too literally by some
who have attempted to illustrate Wagner's conception. But at least it may be said that Wagner himself had the courage of his conviction in this matter, as we learn from an engaging and little-known
recollection that his son, the late Siegfried Wagner,
included in the course of some memoirs of his own
youth. "I remember," wrote Siegfried, "that once
in Vienna, near the end of my father's life, Liszt,
on the occasion of his last meeting with my father,
played Beethoven's Seventh Symphony on the piano.
This led to an incident that produced a very merry
effect upon us children. While Liszt was playing in
the music-room, surrounded by a group of listeners
including my mother and a few friends, we children
listened from without. Suddenly, when Liszt came
to the Scherzo of the Symphony, we saw our father
enter the room, and, unnoticed by Liszt or his
hearers, break into a most skilful dance—one would

have thought that he was a youth of twenty. It was all we could do to keep from betraying our pleasure by delighted laughter. One thing, I am convinced, is certain: Beethoven himself could not have imagined his Scherzo danced more effectively; and Isadora Duncan might well have appealed to my father's example when people objected because she danced to Beethoven's music."

Let us concede that Beethoven might not have objected to the spectacle of Richard Wagner (who worshipped Beethoven beyond all other masters) interpreting in this way the music of the Seventh Symphony. But what would Beethoven have thought and said about certain of the other distinguished interpreters who have sought to tell us in words what this symphony expresses? Would he have been pleased, for instance, by Schumann's assertion that the second movement, the Allegretto, portrays the marriage ceremony of a village couple? Or by d'Ortigue's fancy that this same movement pictures a procession in an old cathedral or in the catacombs? Or by the notion of Dürenberg—a gentleman of far livelier and more exotic fancy—who discovered in this Allegretto what he called "the love-dream of a sumptuous odalisque"?

There have been other and equally discordant

[84]

readings. Marx, for example, discerned in the Symphony as a whole a tale of Moorish knighthood. Teetgen found in it pictures suggested by Scott's *Ivanhoe*. Oulibicheff thought that the music pictured scenes from a masquerade. Lenz and Seroff, two other Russians, found it brilliant with military pomp.

Some later writers on Beethoven—the irreplaceable Philip Hale, for instance—recommended Berlioz's famous interpretation as "the noblest and most poetic appreciation" of this symphony. But that incorruptible Victorian, Sir George Grove, flung the epithet "outrageous" at poor Berlioz's head for daring to say that the first movement of the Seventh Symphony represents a peasants' dance.

The late Vincent d'Indy, composer, scholar, essayist, who wrote with unusual sympathy concerning Beethoven's music, had no patience at all with any of these interpretations. He was quite certain that the Seventh Symphony, like the Sixth, is what he called "a pastoral symphony pure and simple." In the rhythm of the first movement, he declared, "there is certainly nothing dance-like; it seems rather to have been inspired by the song of a bird." He repeated the assertion of the Abbé Stadler that the trio of the Scherzo is an old Pilgrim hymn of Lower

Austria; and he thought that the Finale is a village festival aptly characterized. What the Allegretto represents, Monsieur d'Indy neglected, unfortunately, to tell us.

❦   ❦   ❦

We need not wonder, after all, what Beethoven would have said of all this, for we know what he *did* say of an interpreter scarcely more fantastically imaginative than Schumann or Dürenberg or Marx. Some years after the composition of the Seventh Symphony, a certain Dr. Carl Iken, of Bremen, conceived the idea of helping the public to an understanding of Beethoven's music by devising programmatic interpretations of the symphonies. In the Seventh Symphony, the keen-eyed Doctor discerned, surprisingly enough, the tone-picture of a political revolution. The remarkable program that he invented for the music ran, in part, as follows:

"The sign of revolt is given; there is a rushing and running about of the multitude; an innocent man, or party, is surrounded, overpowered after a struggle, and haled before a judge. Innocence weeps; the judge pronounces a harsh sentence; sympathetic voices mingle in laments and denunciations

—they are those of widows. In the second part of the first movement, the parties have become equal in numbers, and the forces of the law are now scarcely able to quiet the wild tumult. The uprising is suppressed, but the people are not quieted. However, hope smiles cheeringly, and suddenly the voice of the people pronounces the decision in harmonious agreement . . . In the last movement, the classes and the masses mix in a tumultuous picture of unrestrained revelry. The Quality still speak aloofly in the wind instruments. There is a strange bacchantic madness in related chords. We are now on a sunny hill, anon on a flowering meadow, where, in merry May, all the jubilating children of Nature sing with joyful voices."

Richly amusing as this incredible nonsense may seem to us, we can hardly wonder that it infuriated Beethoven, and that he protested energetically. If expositions of his works were necessary, he said, they should be limited to characterization of the music in general terms.

❀   ❀   ❀

Beethoven's Seventh has in our time been called "the most beautiful symphony in the world." Brave words, indeed! and possibly they are justified; though some of us may give ear to the rival claims of other symphonies—the Ninth, perhaps, with its transfigured slow movement. But who shall say which is the "most beautiful" of all symphonies?

Yet perhaps even those who are made uneasy by the positive use of mighty words will hesitate to dispute the special persuasiveness of the music of this Seventh Symphony. One fancies, listening to it, that George Herbert might have imagined something not unlike it when he wrote the line: "My free soul may use her wing." This music has the deathless charm of all music that is unvexed, spontaneous, perfectly released—the flight of wild swans across an Autumn sky, the ripple of wind-swept corn, a gale through April woods, the running of mountain water. Beethoven patterned after Nature in setting his rhythms to a varying pace. This music seems at times as if it were full of the ecstasy of some prehuman beings, responsive to the rapture of the vernal earth; at other times it moves with the grave pace of a commemorative rite, evoking an elegiacal and mournful beauty, as though a curtain were being dropped upon some great and solemn ritual.

But, in the end, we shall be detained, perhaps, not so much by the question of what this symphony "means" (if it has any meaning at all except a purely musical one) as by its mysterious and living changefulness, its possession of that power which I spoke of at the start: the capacity for endless rebirth and self-renewal. The great creators—composers, poets, artists—have known how to outwit dissolution. The truths that were true for them need not be our truths. Often they are not. The point is the degree to which, in them, the depths were stirred, the intensity with which the spirit flamed. Dante survives his cosmos, and Bach his unexamined faith, and Wagner his dialectics, and Blake his glorious insanities (as many chose to call them). But they survive these things, not merely because they are great artists, masters of structure and of style, but because their art bears the irremovable sign of their intensity. Since all creation is a miracle, the flame mysteriously outlasts the fuel; and on the heights the fire glows unceasingly.

THE NINTH

In the world of music, if not in the affairs of nations, the stars in their courses have fought on the side of Demos. It is to Beethoven the commoner that lovers of symphonic music pay their deepest reverence, as to a reader of the minds and hearts of men, a great initiate and master of the spiritual life. And it is in that work whose content is most significant and universal, the Choral Symphony, that he speaks to the music lovers of today with an eloquence that increases with the years. This greatest of all symphonies stands apart from every other work of musical art because it holds within itself the secret patterns of men's futures, and their unpredictable advance. No possible modernity could ever make it seem old-fashioned; for it has passed beyond the power of chance and fate, and has become an all-embracing matrix of the world comprised within our visions and our dreams.

❧   ❧   ❧

Beethoven's completion of the prodigious work in February, 1824, had cheered his spirits, and had set him free for a while from his always agonizing labors over the composition of his music. He no longer grudged himself occasional recreation. Once more he might have been observed on his promenades in Vienna, greeting his friends and acquaintances, and gazing into the shop windows through eyeglasses which, when not in use, dangled at the end of a black ribbon.

Between the completion of his First Symphony and the final scoring of the Ninth, a quarter of a century had elapsed, and Beethoven, having piled masterpieces mountain-high in the lap of the nineteenth century, was within three years of that terrible March evening when he shook his clenched fist at the lightning that blazed into his room, and died to a thunderous obbligato of cosmic timpani—the most stupendous funeral music that ever ushered a genius out of the troubling world.

❁   ❁   ❁

The Ninth Symphony was performed for the first time three months after its completion—at Vienna, on May 7, 1824. It must have been stirring, even for Beethoven's fellow townsmen, to read this line on the official announcement of the concert:

Mr. Ludwig van Beethoven will himself participate in the general direction.

The momentous novelty, announced as a "Grand Symphony with Solo and Choral Voices entering in the Finale on Schiller's Ode to Joy," was the third number on the program. The concert began at seven in the evening. The theatre was crowded in every part—although the Imperial Family may have been laying a cornerstone elsewhere, for the Royal Box was empty. When Beethoven appeared, the audience fixed its attention upon the stocky and compelling figure in a black dress-coat and waistcoat, white neckerchief, black satin small-clothes, black silk stockings, shoes with buckles. That, at least, is Thalberg's description. According to Schindler, however, Beethoven wore a green coat. Schindler, who called for him just before the concert, remarked consolingly, "The theatre will be dark, and no one will notice it.

Michael Umlauf conducted the performance. Schindler has left us a report of the music's effect on its first hearers:

"Never in my life," he wrote, "did I hear such frenetic applause. Once, the second movement of the Symphony [the Scherzo] was completely interrupted by applause, and there was a demand for a repetition. The reception was more than imperial— for the people burst out in a storm four times. At the last there were cries of 'Vivat!' . . . When the parterre broke out in acclamations for the fifth time, the Police Commissioner shouted 'Silence!' "

No wonder the police were disturbed: three successive bursts of applause were the rule for the Imperial Family, and Beethoven, who was only a genius, got five.

❧ ❧ ❧

The deaf Beethoven, engrossed in his score, was wholly unaware of the excitement at the close of the performance.[4] The tale of the incident that followed has become one of the classic Beethoven anecdotes, but it is so touching and dramatic that it remains unstaled. Beethoven, though his place was in the midst of the orchestra, heard nothing whatever of the music. The orchestra and the singers had been warned that although Beethoven would indicate the tempo, the performers must pay no heed to him, but must watch instead the official conductor, Umlauf. At the end of the symphony, Beethoven, his back to the audience, was still turning over the leaves of his score, not knowing that the music had ceased, and that the audience was wildly applauding him. Fräulein Unger, who had

[4] Or after the Scherzo. The accounts differ on this point.

sung the contralto part in the quartet, induced him to turn and face the audience, who were still clapping excitedly and manifesting the greatest enthusiasm. "Beethoven turned around; and the sudden conviction thereby forced upon everyone that he had not done so before because he could not hear what was going on, acted like an electric shock on all present, and a volcanic explosion of sympathy and admiration followed. This was repeated again and again, and seemed as though it would never end."

Two years after, in the Autumn of 1826, Beethoven sent a letter to the King of Prussia in which he assured that gentleman of his great happiness in being permitted to dedicate a certain work to His Majesty. Beethoven was fortunate enough, he declared, to count himself—"as a citizen of Bonn"— amongst His Majesty's subjects, and he begged the King to accept the work as what he called "a trifling token" of the high reverence which he gave to all His Majesty's virtues.

The so-called "trifling token" was the score of the Ninth Symphony. The King was that Prussian tory, Friedrich Wilhelm III, then an ardent disciple of Prince Metternich. The King's response was most amiable. "In view of the recognized worth of your compositions," he was so gracious as to say,

"I was much pleased at receiving the new work which you have sent me. I thank you for this gift, and hand you the accompanying diamond ring as a token of my sincere appreciation." When the gift was received and examined by Beethoven, it proved to be not a diamond ring at all, but one set with what Schindler contemptuously calls "a reddish stone," which an expert reported to be worth three hundred florins in paper money.

Poor Beethoven—a bogus diamond ring and a patronizing letter in return for the Ninth Symphony!

❦   ❦   ❦

Was there a poetic scheme in Beethoven's mind, relating to the Ninth Symphony as a whole, which persuaded him of the logic of attaching to the three instrumental movements a choral setting of Schiller's Ode to Joy? Certain critical commentators on Beethoven have scouted this idea. They warn us that we are not justified in seeking to discover any poetic interrelation between the first three movements of the Choral Symphony and the Ode to Joy which inspired its Finale. They ask us to believe that the Symphony as a whole has no meaning other than a musical one: that the Choral Finale, with its setting of Schiller's Ode, is merely a sort of musico-poetic accident, without reference to the significance of the work as a unit.

Sir George Grove, for example, remarks that "the very title of the work—Beethoven's own—is conclusive on this point. It is not a 'Symphony on Schiller's Ode to Joy'; but it is a 'Symphony with Final Chorus on Schiller's Ode to Joy'—*Sinfonie mit Schluss-Chor über Schillers Ode an die Freude.* . . . The first three movements," Sir George continues, "might have had another Finale [5]—indeed, they nearly had one; and it is not necessary to attempt to reconcile either the opening Allegro, the Scherzo (so called) or the Adagio, with the train of thought and feeling suggested by the Ode which is embodied in the latter portion of the work. . . ."

The bland assumption that "it is not necessary to attempt to reconcile" the several parts of a presumably organic work of art has always struck some

[5] The distinguished musicologist, Max Unger, pointed out in a thoughtful article in *The Musical Quarterly* for July, 1938, that sketches for the Ninth Symphony indicate that "Beethoven went about for a long time with the intention of finding a place in the final movement for a—waltz." Perhaps that is not so astonishing as Herr Unger seems to think. Waltz rhythms are not necessarily incompatible with a great work. There is one, for example, in Tristan's death scene, in Wagner's music-drama; and the Choral Finale of the Ninth Symphony might conceivably have employed the rhythm of a waltz without disturbing us by any sense of incongruity.

[96]

of us as an astonishing exhibition of aesthetic irre-
sponsibility. We are still awaiting, from those who
espouse this strangely frivolous thesis, an explanation that will make it clear how any work of art
could possibly be coherent if its different parts were
irreconcilable as members of an imaginative whole.

Some of these commentators have pointed out
that the Symphony is integrated musically, and its
unity of design established, by the intervallic simi-
larity of certain of its themes. This is true enough,
so far as it goes. But it does not dispose of the
deeper question of the Symphony's spiritual and
poetical unity. *That* question will not down. We are
obliged to seek more than a musical meaning in the
Symphony as a whole because its composer has
plainly invited us to do so—unless we are willing
to admit that the work is a gigantic hybrid, a mix-
ture of species, three-fourths absolute music and
one-fourth cantata, with no unifying spiritual pattern to give it meaning and coherence.

One of the persons who seem to have disagreed
with the commentators in this matter was Beethoven
himself; for there are indications in his sketchbooks

that he looked both backward and forward during his last year of work on the score, seeing the beginning in the end and the end in the beginning. There is reason to believe that the Symphony is held together by some unifying poetic principle, some spiritual cord which threads it, in Shankara's phrase, "like the string in a chain of pearls."

Thayer reminds us in his authoritative biography that "serious and continuous labor upon the Symphony was not taken up until after the completion of the *Missa Solemnis*." That is to say, Beethoven's period of concentration upon the Symphony (though its roots are to be found much earlier in his creative life) "began in 1822, covered the greater part of 1823, and ended in the early part of 1824." Beethoven, therefore, as Thayer concludes, "worked on the Symphony a little more than a year."

It is in his sketchbooks of the year 1823 that we shall find what some regard as confirmation of the reassuring belief that the Ninth Symphony is not a tonal hybrid, but a spiritually and poetically integrated whole. By grouping certain of the sketches over which Beethoven agonized while trying to establish a verbal link between the instrumental movements and the Choral Finale, the conviction emerges that the Symphony is, after all, a continuous imaginative texture. Sir Donald Tovey, one of the most scholarly and searching students of Beethoven's creative mind, has drawn our attention [6] to the fact that Beethoven himself gives us clews wherefrom we can evolve "an account of the first three movements of the Symphony."

After remarking that "the general scheme of the whole symphony as a setting for Schiller's 'Ode to Joy' is simple and satisfactory enough," Tovey continues:

"The first movement gives us the tragedy of life. The second movement gives us the reaction from tragedy to a humor never purely joyful except in a childhood which is itself pathetic when contemplated from that distance of time at which alone it can be appreciated. The slow movement is beauty of an order too sublime for a world of action; it has no action, and its motion is that of the stars in their courses. . . .

"Now we shall find that this account of the first three movements of the Ninth Symphony is Beethoven's own; and the Ninth Symphony is not the first work in which he had attempted something

[6] In a pamphlet containing an analysis of the Ninth Symphony prepared for the concerts of the Reid Orchestra of Edinburgh; afterward published, in an altered form, in Tovey's masterly *Essays in Musical Analysis* (Oxford University Press, 1935).

of the kind, a search for a theme on which the mind could rest as a final solution of typical human doubts and difficulties. . . .

"In the Ninth Symphony, Beethoven's plan is to remind us of the first three movements just as they have been described above; and to reject them one by one as failing to attain the joy in which he believes. After all three have been rejected, a new theme is to appear, and that theme shall be hailed and sung as the Hymn of Joy. Beethoven's first idea was that a baritone should express all this process in words, from the outset, in an impassioned recitative. The orchestra was to start with a confused din expressing terror and violence, the singer was to rebuke it, whereupon the orchestra was to give out the opening of the first three movements, after each of which the singer was to point out that it was not to the purpose; until, on the appearance of the new theme, the singer accepted it with triumph and set it to Schiller's ode. Beethoven sketched all the recitative with the necessary words. . . . [He] soon saw that he had better commit himself to the smallest amount of plain prose that could possibly suffice. . . . Let the basses of the orchestra seem on the point of articulate speech with their passionate recitative. Everything is there without words."

Beethoven's descriptive key words may be studied in the sketchbooks.[7] They are deeply suggestive and revealing. How illuminating, for example, are the words written at the point where the melody of the Adagio is recalled: "Nor this . . . it is too tender."

❁   ❁   ❁

The four incomparable movements tower among the peaks of the musical imagination. The beetling first Allegro, with its crushing impartment of a tragic poet's sense of the darkness and terror that surround all human destiny, is the most tremendous thing that Beethoven ever wrote. This music, with its sinister immensities, rises threateningly before us after the ominous mystery of the opening measures.

Toward the end of the movement we seem to come upon a tonal anticipation of that Dark Tower of Childe Roland's encounter in the perturbing and terrible poem of Browning. But this crisis, this catastrophe, that looms behind the portents of Beethoven's orchestra, is not to be thought of in terms of mere external tone-painting: this is a catastrophe of the spirit, a tragedy remote from the mate-

[7] See Thayer, Vol. III, pp. 149, 150.

rial world, austere and lonely and incommunicable.

The so-called Scherzo, that gigantic spout of life, is an apotheosis of rhythmic energy unequalled even among the achievements of the supreme master of torrential symphonic speech.

In the ineffable slow movement, Beethoven is living and breathing in a region beyond the world of sense and change. The composer of this trans-figured music reminds us of what the wife of Beethoven's contemporary, the poet and visionary, William Blake, said of her husband while they lived together—that one saw little of him, "because he was so often away in Paradise." A superearthly beauty rests upon these unapproachable measures. Beethoven the tone-poet is doubled here by Beethoven the seer, knowing things that we know not, having a lamp that we have lost, piercing the gulfs beyond the circling world—yet realizing poignantly that these beatitudes exceed the reach of living men. Yet, for a moment of divine felicity, the dreamer transcends the old bewilderment of earthly strife. The healing essence of assuaging loveliness has stilled his pain, and made it seem unreal until the paradisal vision fades.

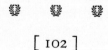

But what a blaze of light and what a tumult of the morning stars, what music of awe and ecstasy and tenderness, Beethoven gives us in the Finale, with its choral setting of Schiller's Ode to Joy! At the close of this movement and of the symphony, Beethoven, towering and superhuman, seems truly to be shouting with irrepressible jubilation among the choiring suns of space. In this outpouring of rapturous exultation, Beethoven's singers become priests and priestesses of a new and preposterous religion of human brotherhood and human love, summoning a vision of our mortal destiny so restorative and clear that only the very simple and the very wise believe in it. Beethoven, one of the simplest and most profoundly wise of men, believed in the reality of which he dreamed, and he dared to sing of it. The Symphony's Finale is his vision made actual for our imaginations. Here is that outpouring of radiance and warmth, that limitless expansion of our awareness, implied in Beethoven's sublime illusion of a lovelier and more generous world. It is the testament of Beethoven the singer and the seer, chanting beneath a sky reverberant with many voices (as of mortals bright with immortality) his mighty song of the comradeship of man.

It is impossible not to know what Beethoven means when he lifts his voice and stretches forth his hands in this enormous jubilation. We know that this is music unspeakably fortifying, enlarging, releasing—music that unbinds the shackled and gives wings to the infirm. We know that here, in this horizonless extension of ourselves, we and our brothers have become unbelievably one. We know that this is music of faith as well as of transport, infinitely quickening and sustaining. Hearing it, we know that in the presence of this life-giving music no disability or narrowness of spirit can survive: that in the company of these joyous, chanting hosts, of whom we have become mysteriously a part, the lame may leap and the dumb may sing.

No wonder the generations have said of such an artist, in the magnificent phrase of the Upanishads, "He builds for endlessness."

❁   ❁   ❁

Perhaps only those who approach the mysteries of Beethoven's imaginative world with simplicity of spirit, with genius, and with awe can give us a true sense of the special quality of the Ninth—its strange blend of fatefulness and transport, its wild humor and supermundane beauty, its tragical despair, and its shouting among the stars.

Since Toscanini first conducted the Ninth Symphony in America, in the year before the World War, he has repeatedly proved to us that he is the unique interpreter of this work. His realizing of the first movement, with its hugeness of menace and catastrophe, exhausts the contents of the music. In the celestial slow movement he searches the living heart of Beethoven. The essential beauty of this movement is an efflorescence of tranquillized and sublimated song. Upon its release for the ear and the imagination depends the creation of the music's spell. Beethoven has given us here the choicest treas-ure of his score. This is its inmost spirit and its perfected voice. To re-create the beauty of such music in its fullness and its purity is an act of perfect faith and of transcendent genius. But specifically it is a matter almost wholly of the just and affectionate moulding of Beethoven's cantilena, that cantilena which at first is grave and unadorned, and afterward exquisitely ornate, with its garlanding fioriture which have the dignity and purity of mobile sculpture, ceaselessly fluent and alive.

Always, with Toscanini, we hear this music's voice. In phrasing, in rhythmic pulse, in the difficult sustainment of a mood, its evocation is subduing and complete. And when he has come to the end of the Choral Finale, those stupendous pages in which Beethoven dares to show us an unborn world of light and liberation, of love without human barriers or limitations, we realize that the re-creator has stood throughout at the creator's side, at one with his vision and his faith.

❀　　❀　　❀

How are such things achieved? It is no easier to say at this late day than it has ever been. Perhaps one might conjecture that they are achieved only through the possession of some such capacity for assimilation as that of which De Sanctis spoke in praising Dante—"the gift of steeping the soul in the thing, which is the secret of life, of love, and of genius."

THE "MISSA SOLEMNIS"

Toward the end of August, in the year 1819, Beethoven's devoted friend and biographer, Anton Schindler, went to call upon Ludwig at his country home in Mödling, accompanied by an acquaintance.

"It was 4 o'clock in the afternoon," wrote Schindler. . . . "In the living room, behind a locked door, we heard the master singing, howling, stamping. After we had been listening a long time to this almost awful scene, and were about to go away, the door opened and Beethoven stood before us with distorted features, calculated to excite fears. . . . Never, it may be said, did so great an art-work see its creation under more adverse circumstances."

It was the *Missa Solemnis* by which Beethoven was thus possessed. We need not wonder at his agitation. In addition to his labors on the Mass, Beethoven was in bad health, he was distraught by personal difficulties of various kinds, and, as though he were not sufficiently occupied by the task of composing the most formidable religious score since the B minor Mass of Bach, he had lately been making arduous side trips into the difficult uplands of the Ninth Symphony.

❧　❧　❧

Perhaps the essential thing that should be noted about the *Missa Solemnis* is that it is more than a traditional setting of the words of the Mass. It was intended originally for use in connection with the installation of Beethoven's friend and pupil, the Archduke Rudolf, as Archbishop of Olmütz, in 1820. But it was not finished in time for that occasion; and long before the score was completed, Beethoven's passionate and dramatizing imagination had overleaped all the bounds of institutional traditions and liturgical formulas, and had gone its own imperious way. For Beethoven, as he proceeded in his setting of the ancient and marvellous words, responded more and more unrestrainedly to their emotional and imaginative suggestions, fixing his attention less on the churchly rubrics, on ecclesiastical or ceremonial decorum, than on the human implications of the missal text. He remembered the grievous, unconquerable souls of men, suffering, fearing, longing, pleading, hoping, worshipping, praying. And at the thought of the timeless drama of human agony and aspiration, the sanctuary opened before his all-embracing vision and became the peopled earth and all mankind, and above them was a strangely echoing sky.

Indeed, it could be said of Beethoven in this universal and compassionate music, as it has been said of St. Francis, that his imagination did not falter "until it held the world."

The dominant characteristic of Beethoven's

music for the Mass is its extraordinary intensity and immediacy of musical speech: it is the most intimately personal utterance in the great religious music of the world.

Bach, in his B minor Mass, speaks to us with the sublimated voice of Christendom in the presence of the mysteries and terrors and ecstasies of men's souls.

But in Beethoven's Mass the anguish and aspiration and exaltation of the believer are still personal, still concentrated in the idealized image of the human being whose testament this music is. The drama, its passions and ardors and transmutations, are enacted almost before our eyes.

❀   ❀   ❀

The superb performances of the Mass to which Toscanini has accustomed us in America are likely to make us forget how cruelly difficult this music is. It is not only difficult to sing; it is difficult in other ways—in the problems of style and of imaginative comprehension that it sets before its interpreters; in its strange blend of rapt spirituality and human drama. In the Dona Nobis, for example, the menacing drum-beats, the warlike trumpet calls, the anguished voices that cry for peace, baffled many early hearers of the work, who did not realize that Beethoven was giving them here a musical symbolization of the endless conflict between the world and the spirit, between man and his enemies without and within. In this music, at its most impassioned and dramatic, Beethoven recalls the fervor and simplicity of the Middle Ages, and shows us drama in the service of religious experience, as a symbol of the spirit's intensest life.

Beethoven's French biographer, the late Vincent d'Indy—himself a composer of noble and devout imagination—believed that in the presence of Beethoven's Mass in D we stand before a work with which only the B minor Mass of Bach and the *Parsifal* of Wagner can be compared. And indeed this Opus 123 of Beethoven is music of exceeding greatness. No wonder Beethoven raved and agonized as it was born of him, crying out in anguish while it was taking shape in his mind and on his music paper. Those who were about him at the time say also that he "seemed to be transfigured by it." He had the meaning of the Latin words of the text minutely explained to him, with their proper accentuation. For almost five years he dwelt with them, filled with the anguish of parturition, but also with the ecstasy that must have sustained him as sheet after sheet of the marvellous score passed across his desk; and then one day he set down the last note, and on the manuscript of the Kyrie he wrote the simple and characteristic words: "From the heart—may it go to the heart!"

❀   ❀   ❀

Although Beethoven composed the Mass while the Ninth Symphony was germinating in his mind (the Symphony was begun before and finished after the *Missa Solemnis*), the two works are strikingly different in style. The melodic and harmonic texture of the Choral Symphony is characterized, for the most part, by its lofty plainness and directness and simplicity, and by its prevailingly diatonic character. But these traits are not the distinguishing ones of the *Missa Solemnis*. Here Beethoven speaks in a different tongue, in language far more piercing and intense, far more subjective, more in the vein of the last string quartets. The melodic line is more flexible, more subtly moulded; the harmony of certain passages is of an astonishing modernity.

The Beethoven whom we meet in the greater pages of the *Missa Solemnis* foreshadows the Beethoven of the last phase, Beethoven the brooding and clairvoyant dreamer, the self-communing seer.

As we sit before the Prelude to the Benedictus in the Mass, with its hushed and rapt and fathomless contemplation—in which, as d'Indy said, Beethoven has raised silence into sublimity—we know that this is the ultimate and essential Beethoven: that we have plumbed as deeply as we shall ever get to the mystery of a great spirit. We know that for this tragical and passionate dreamer, so simple of heart, so racked by the task of living and by the spectacle of human conflict and frustration, this music of boundless tenderness and pity was a solvent and a miraculous release. We know that, as he set it down, the prophecy of Isaiah must have come true for his turbulent and baffled spirit, and that the eyes of the blind were opened, and the ears of the deaf unstopped.

❧   ❧   ❧

The *Missa Solemnis* has been known in America for more than half a century; but it would scarcely be rash to say that the imaginative and musical significance of the work had never been fully disclosed until its first performances under Toscanini's consecrational leadership—performances of surpassing intensity and power and dedicatory fervor, inspired by the most searching and impassioned penetration into the depths of Beethoven's meaning, and by a fanaticism of devotion and aesthetic faith that transformed the materials with which it dealt, and turned them into vehicles of revelation.

It is not enough for Toscanini that the words, "Kyrie eleison," be understood by his singers in their obvious and surface meaning. The burning imagination of the leader pierces to the timeless reality within and behind the words, behind Beethoven's tragical setting, and kindles his artists with a sense of that reality. Toscanini is aware that the task of the interpreter in any art is to reveal the stress and passion within the core of each expressive moment, so that at last the presented vision of pity or of grief, tenderness or faith, shall awaken in us the feeling of "that unavoidable solidarity in mysterious origin, in joy, in hope, in uncertain fate, which binds men to each other and all mankind to the visible world."

It is merely another one of the countless evidences of Toscanini's genius as an interpreter that he feels so deeply the personal and human quality in the *Missa Solemnis.* He makes us realize, for example, that the lament of Beethoven's Crucifixus is a different thing from the otherworldly sorrow of Bach, the sorrow of a brooding and compassionate god. Beethoven's lamentation proceeds from a different area of the imagination. It springs from an emotion incomparably intimate and vivid; it is the issue of a thing experienced in the flesh, remembered with ancestral anguish through centuries of incredulous grief.

❦   ❦   ❦

Such performances as these lay bare for us, with unapproachable clarity and eloquence, the inner life and the secret intensities of a master's piercing vision of the tragedy and piteousness of man and the miracle of his faith. So that we are left, toward the end, as the voices breathe their affecting "Pacem . . . pacem" in that final exquisite recurrence of Beethoven's seraphic cantilena, with a profound conviction that we have experienced "that subtle but invincible conviction of solidarity," as Conrad called it, "which knits together the loneliness of innumerable hearts, the dead to the living, the living to the unborn." One thinks of the dead but ever-living

Beethoven, and of those hovering phrases, with their ineffable tenderness and beauty, which must have brought to him, when he conceived them, such a benison of assuagement as his poor deaf ears had ever known . . . "So also," he might have whispered to himself, "are the wings of the spirit over my heart."

IV

SCHUBERT IN EXCELSIS

"I HOPE to be able to send you," wrote Mendelssohn to the London Philharmonic Society a
century ago, "a very extraordinary and excellent
symphony by Fr. Schubert, the famous composer."
The symphony in question, "extraordinary and excellent" indeed, was Schubert's last, in C major.[1]
But when the worthy players of the London Philharmonic tried over the new work at rehearsal some
years later, under Mendelssohn's direction, they
seem to have found it merely amusing, and they
laughed so immoderately at the reiterated triplet
figure in the Finale that Mendelssohn, incensed,
withdrew the symphony from performance. It is not
recorded that when this symphony was performed
for the first time in America, in 1851, the players

[1] There is an earlier and lesser symphony by Schubert in the
same key.

found anything to laugh at in the Finale. Probably, by that time, those rushing, tumultuous triolets had ceased to be funny and had become sublime.

The manuscript of the symphony is dated by Schubert, "March, 1828." He himself never heard it. Eight months after he finished it, on November 14th, he took to his bed; and at three o'clock in the afternoon of Wednesday, November 19, 1828, —as Sir George Grove wrote in his touching narrative—"Schubert breathed his last, and his simple, earnest soul took its flight from the world. He was thirty-one years, nine months, and nineteen days old. There never has been one like him, and there never will be another."

❀   ❀   ❀

It is the conviction of many students and music lovers that this symphony contains the greatest music that Schubert ever wrote; and there is, for them, a certain comfort in the thought that Schubert—the simple-minded, tongue-tied, poverty-stricken musician who died so miserably—should have been able to say his last symphonic word in music that is so prodigally full of strength and joy and radiance, music that is the very voice of lyric ecstasy, unloosed and jubilant: music that seems to have issued from the dayspring of the world and the rapture of the first dawn. If ever the human spirit shook itself free from earthly bonds and impediments, outsoaring poverty and wretchedness, defying time and death, it was on the day that Schubert conceived the tumultuous glory of the Finale of this symphony—which surely must have been written at a single sitting, in a sacred fury of inspiration.

For let us not forget the privations of Schubert's life and the obscurity and wretchedness of his end. When he died, he left behind him personal effects valued at a little over twelve dollars (reckoning in our money). A few coats, waistcoats, trousers, shirts, cravats, handkerchiefs, socks, one hat, one towel, one sheet, one mattress, one bolster, one quilt, and a quantity of manuscripts appraised by the official inventory at the present equivalent of about two dollars—that was the extent of his material possessions. Within a year of his death he had been unable to afford a seventeen-cent dinner, and he was selling immortal songs for what would amount to approximately twenty cents apiece. As Sir George Grove observed, with justifiable bitterness, "beside this, the poverty of Mozart—the first of the two great musicians whom Vienna has allowed to starve—was wealth."

Yet Schubert, in the midst of this wretchedness, turned out masterworks with staggering casualness. "When I have done one piece I begin the next," he remarked simply to a visitor. In one morning he wrote six of the songs in the *Winterreise*. He composed nearly a thousand works in thirteen years; and "at the age when Beethoven had produced one symphony," as Sir George observes, "Schubert had written nine."

❧   ❧   ❧

His last symphony was the supreme anomaly of his life. Earth-bound and wretched as a man, he was free and triumphant as an artist; and the music of this final symphony proceeds in clarity and light, wind-borne, under a wind-swept sky.

Where else shall one find music with a comparable energy and pace and high exuberance, traversing a lyric world of cloudless sun, "leaping and shining like a mountain water"?—and the mountain is in the country of the gods.

Yet Schubert, the human being, could one of us have beheld him, would have seemed a good deal

less than godlike. He was an insignificant little man.
He stood five feet one inch in his socks. He was
awkward and stoop-shouldered. He had a snub nose.
His large head seemed too heavy for his body. He
was painfully shortsighted, and his spectacles seldom
left his face. Often he was shy and silent and em-
barrassed. The boundless eloquence of the musician
found no echoes in the man. Schubert was never a
talker, says one of his biographers. "He could not
talk well, and he seems to have been aware of this
defect. He could talk on nothing save music, and
then he seldom spoke until someone had dropped
badly on a wrong note. He would sit, smoking a
pipe, grinning, nodding his head, his face a mask.
Nor could he enter into argument or refute criticism. The retorts that often sprang into his mind
were seldom spoken. He became secretive, inarticulate. When irritated, he spoke in short sentences,
or took refuge in the Viennese expression, 'Wurz!'
(Nonsense!) Or he would utter a brief and cutting
sarcasm in some Viennese colloquialism. He seemed
indifferent to praise; his friend Schindler says that
he never saw Schubert's expression change when
compliments were paid him."

Schubert's comrade, Holzapfel, the paralytic,
used to talk endlessly of the friend whom he had

known, and always he began his reminiscences in the same way: "He was a very little man, but he was a giant."

❦　　❦　　❦

If Schubert had written nothing but this symphony in C major, his head would be among the stars.

In this music, the discourse, almost throughout, is like that of a speaker who knows and loves and cunningly employs "the shape and hue and odor and sweet sound of words." It is full of surprising and inexhaustible subtleties of design and procedure, of delicate felicities accomplished with so perfect an art that they wear the innocence and spontaneity of natural processes. Consider, as one example among many, a detail in the slow movement even more delectable than that famous incident which so captivated the romantic Schumann, the passage in which "the horn is calling as though . . . from another sphere": consider that place (it is in the twenty-fourth measure from the opening of the Andante con moto, where the song of the oboe unfolding the main theme passes from A minor into A major, and begins the lovely subsidiary that follows it. Nothing, apparently, could be simpler, more unsought, than that change from minor to major; yet how consummately artful it is, and how ravishing! And mark the touch of magic—seemingly naïve—that is given further on to the second theme by the D-flat in the 'cellos.

When one thinks of the larger aspects of this score—not of its endless felicity of detail, but of the tireless strength and grandeur of its line and progress—it is tempting to wonder if the Winged Victory did not, in the mind of its creator, breast the winds to music such as the Finale of this symphony. Even those who are not informed musicians must be stirred and uplifted by this culminating movement. If this Finale is not the pure, brave ecstasy of tone, then that ecstasy was never captured and released by a composer. One remembers Francis Thompson's praise of Shelley's *Prometheus Unbound:* "that amazing lyric world," he called it, "where the very grass is all a-rustle with lovely spirit things, where poetry is spilt like wine, and music runs to drunken waste. The choruses sweep down the wind, tirelessly, flight after flight, till the breathless soul almost cries for respite from the unrolling splendors."

Like all authentic masterworks, the C major Symphony has an ever-receding horizon. It gives us the sense of an enchanted familiarity: that sense of both the wonder and the intimacy of the world—the conviction that just beyond the next hill lies some accessible paradise for the pilgrim mind. To create and maintain that illusion is surely to conquer, by the most daring of flights, a boundless region of the kingdoms of the spirit.

❀   ❀   ❀

If any symphony could challenge the C minor of Brahms for second place after the monarch of them all, Beethoven's Ninth, it would surely be this symphony of Schubert's. Toscanini, within recent years in America, has made the work peculiarly his own. He seems to understand it, as he understands so many other kinds of music, with an unmatched penetration of its special quality. He reminds us that Schubert in this symphony is both simple and sublime. Schubert's simplicities have not the profundity of Beethoven's, but they have a sublimity that is their own; and in the last movement they speak with an elemental grandeur that must quicken the breath of anyone who listens with sensibility.

It has been said of this movement—Schubert's supreme achievement—that in composing it he had thought of Phaëthon driving Apollo's chariot across the sky. Another and far odder notion was that Schubert in the coda expressed "his fear of death." It may be doubted if Schubert was thinking either of chariots or of fear. If he was thinking of anything but music, it was surely of such things as light and ecstasy and valor, and the orbit of the spirit through eternity.

It is of such liberating concepts that Toscanini makes us think as he releases the empyrean tides of this Finale. The music itself is an apotheosis of rhythmic energy. The momentum of it becomes, under Toscanini's baton, gigantic and irresistible, a dance of constellations in some prehuman dawn.

This stupendous sweep of radiance and jubilation Toscanini brings to us with a blinding veracity that fills up all our sense of the miracle of life; and something leaps within us as Schubert spans the sky, shouting and exulting while he shakes its glory from his wings.

V

THE SYMPHONIC BRAHMS

IT IS probable that most of those for whom the symphonies of Brahms are an indispensable part of their musical experience would find it difficult to believe that there was a time, not long ago, when Brahms was regarded, except by a few devotees here and there, as a composer whose music was hard-shelled, forbidding, and austere. One does not have to be advanced in years to remember when Brahms was looked upon as a composer for the few, for the elect, for a small group of initiates. If anyone at that period had been bold enough to declare that the symphonies of Brahms would soon be almost as popular with the general musical public as the symphonies of Beethoven, and more so than the symphonies of Tchaikovsky, he would certainly have been greeted by a tornado of derisive laughter. But today the laugh is on the scoffers.

The immense popularity of the symphonic Brahms is a matter of comparatively recent growth. It was only a while ago that James Huneker (one of the earliest American connoisseurs of the Olympian Johannes) was begging us in his brilliant and persuasive way to stop thinking of Brahms as harsh and astringent, and insisting that it was really quite possible to love and cherish him. He assured us that beneath the rough exterior of Brahms the composer there beats a human and accessible heart! Even the Perfect Brahmsian among English critics found it necessary, at about the same time, to take account of what he called "the difficulty of grasping this music"—and by "this music" he meant, remarkably enough, the slow movement of the D major Symphony!

SYMPHONY NO. I, IN C MINOR

For many years, most music lovers, musicians, and critics thought of the C minor Symphony in the terms that were frequently applied to it when it was first revealed to the world in 1876—as music repellent and abstruse. Even Hanslick, the Vienna critic who worshipped Brahms, called it "difficult of comprehension."

When Hermann Levi, the famous Wagner con-

ductor, directed the C minor at Munich a year after
its première, the music was hissed. And it was not
the Wagnerites, said Levi, who did the hissing, but
the "classicists," so called. In our own country, a
celebrated critic of an elder day, hearing this symphony in 1878, brushed it aside with sorrowful dis-
approbation. "It will not be loved," he declared,
"like the dear masterpieces of genius."

That, it appears, was a bad guess. For indis-
putably the C minor Symphony of Brahms is now
one of the half dozen most popular works in the
symphonic list. Indubitably great it seems to us
today, music akin to that cleansing and tonic order
of poetry (whether of tones or of words) which,
as Elton said of Wordsworth, "disinfects life for
us," and makes it seem, for a time, restorative and
inexhaustible, magnificently worth the struggle and
weariness and anguish it entails.

Some of us would go so far as to assert that
there is only one Finale in all symphonic literature
—that of Beethoven's Ninth—which transcends in
grandeur of inspiration the last movement of the
C minor Symphony of Brahms, and only one other
Finale, that of Schubert's C major, that is perhaps
its equal. For Brahms at the summit of his powers,

as he is in the concluding movement of his First Symphony, has left us music of a beauty so lofty and renewing, a humanity so all-embracing, and a heroic spirit so insuperable, that Beethoven, one cannot doubt, would have been proud to sign his name to it. Especially in the peroration of this movement, with its apocalyptic splendor of vision and affirmation and its prophetic ecstasy, the music takes us up into the high and lonely places of the spirit's world, and we can never afterward be quite the same again.

❦   ❦   ❦

I suspect that posterity will smile a bit at the expense of an earlier generation when they discover that the real Brahms, this tone-poet of inexhaustible tenderness, this master of spacious and lucid generosities, was once regarded as crabbed, sour, bitter, morose, and unintelligible.

We know that Brahms himself, despite the protective roughness with which he faced the world, was one of the tenderest and kindest of human beings (though he would go to almost any length rather than betray his feelings). And we know that the sensibility and warmth of Brahms the man, the shy and reticent humanitarian, had their equivalent in Brahms the artist, the creator of humane and noble music, the composer of the symphonies, the Requiem, the concertos, the songs, with their depth and truth of feeling, their range of sympathy, their compassionate awareness of the lives and destinies of men—in short, their essential humanity and their universal appeal. The music of Brahms has the fullness and variety of substance, the volume, the power, the greatness of style, the imaginative reach, to justify comparison with the elect. He was a first-rate genius. The mystically daring Emerson might have called him "a Maker." He is full-stored and bountiful. Like Whitman, Brahms the composer could have said, "I am large, I contain multitudes."

❀   ❀   ❀

He was never greater than in his first symphony, that confident masterpiece which, in his middle age, he dared to write, postponing its completion until he felt that he might justifiably essay the form that Beethoven had set upon the heights. He had passed his forty-third birthday when he finished the monumental score. Its confident mastery is evident throughout. From the first notes of this symphony we are aware of a great voice, uttering superb poetic speech. The momentous opening is an exordium that proclaimed a new and individual symphonic speech, an utterance in the grand tradition; and the succeeding Allegro is one of those tonal webs of molten steel that only Brahms could fabricate.

In the deeply probing slow movement we encounter the Brahms of long vistas and grave meditations. How personal in feeling and expression is the whole of this Andante sostenuto! No one but Brahms could have extracted the precise quality of emotion that issues from the simple and heartfelt theme for the strings and bassoon in the opening measures; and the song of the oboe has lured an irreproachably sober commentator into conferring upon it the attribute of "sublimity." Though perhaps "sublimity"—a shy bird, even on Olympus— is to be found not here, but elsewhere in the symphony.

The third movement is beguiling in its own special loveliness; but the chief glory of this symphony is the Finale.

Here, if need be, is an appropriate resting place for that diffident eagle among epithets, Sublimity. Here there are space and air and light to tempt its wings. The wonderful C major song first heard from the horn in the slow introduction is interrupted

by a foreshadowing of the solemn chorale-like phrase
for the trombones and bassoons that halts the breath
by its startling grandeur when it returns as the climax of the movement. And then comes the chief
theme of the Allegro—that ample and heartening
melody which sweeps us onward to the culminating
moment in the Finale: the blinding revelation of the
chorale in the coda, which may recall to some the
luminous prophecy of another seer: "There will
come a time when it shall be light; and when man
shall awaken from his lofty dreams, and find his
dreams still there, and that nothing has gone save
his sleep."

❋　❋　❋

It used to be alleged, by observers of the type
who think in formulas, that Toscanini as a conductor subjected all music to a process that was supposed to make it sound unduly lyrical. "He was held
to 'Italianize' everything he played because he made
all music sound clear and beautiful," remarks an
observer of a different kind, my colleague, Samuel
Chotzinoff (that discerning and persuasive New
Yorker who was instrumental in bringing Toscanini
back to America). "We know now that he is Italian
without being superficial, German without being

heavy and pompous, French without being vague and precious."

This is justly and admirably said. Toscanini has made clear at least one of the reasons why his playing of Brahms—the most Teutonic of masters —has given us a new insight into this music. Perhaps, indeed, the secret of his power of making us hear in a new way all music that passes through his imagination is to be sought in his allegiance to that noble tradition which conceives of music as essential song, whether it be dramatically urgent, heroically broad, or the free and seemingly spontaneous utterance of lyric fervor.

What he does for the C minor Symphony of Brahms is known to the discerning. His conception of the work has long seemed the noblest, the most poetical, the most loftily dramatic that one has heard. From the opening notes of the slow introduction (which he plays at an unusually propulsive and appropriate tempo) one is made aware that nothing is to be taken for granted: that this hackneyed work, the prey of every conductor avid of sure-fire effectiveness, is being bared to us with the recovered ardor of a pristine experience; and that this freshness and fervor are transforming the living body of the music.

Upon every measure of the score, Toscanini wreaks the power of his incandescent imagination, slighting nothing, disdaining perfunctoriness as the cardinal sin, yet never overstressing by a hair's weight the value or the proportional significance of a note or phrase or period.

The issue disables praise. One had not known that the Andante sostenuto (taken at a tempo that seems inevitable in its justness) could be made to yield so rich a loveliness so nobly wrought, with the sentimental lure immeasurably distant, the fervor of the music so intimate and so seizing—the exquisiteness of the third measure, for example; or the manner in which, later, the ascending steplike phrase for the violins is made to sound as it had not done before.

The Adagio of the introduction to the Finale has the tenseness of poetic tragedy: the famous *stringendo* measures are not transformed into a conductor's stunt, but keep their proper place in the scheme of the section. One notes the beautiful and perhaps surprising tenderness of the chorale in the following Più Andante—surprising, unless one had also noted carefully how Brahms has marked the passage. The big tune of the Allegro is neither heavy-footed nor overdriven, but spacious and jocund at once, lustily Brahmsian, "broad as ten thousand beeves at pasture."

But the surpassing moment in this publication of the symphony is the close of the Finale, with its uplifting recurrence of the chorale which unseals the aural vision of those released from sleep.

The passage has always been a stumbling block to conductors; for it has seemed to them that if the chorale were to be proclaimed with adequate effect, the Brahmsian letter must be disregarded, and the notes of the chorale given double the time-value that they have in the score. Most conductors, faced with this predicament, pay no attention to Brahms' instructions, and expand the chorale to twice its written length. Toscanini makes the problem seem unreal. He takes the chorale almost *a tempo*—there is a perceptible slackening of pace, but not enough to halt the jubilant onrush of the music to that climax which is the apex of all symphonic music since the Ninth, with its splendor of revelation and its blaze of pentecostal light.

SYMPHONY NO. 2, IN D MAJOR

Toscanini's procedure with the Second Symphony of Brahms, the D major, is no less enlightening.

This symphony was finished only a year after the completion of the First. According to our present view, contemporaneous comment on the two works seems to have been curiously undiscerning. Half a century ago, in Central Europe, the C minor Symphony was regarded as abstruse, austere, forbidding, and the D major was hailed by many as a grateful relief—as a thing predominantly "sunny," full of happiness and lyric grace. Even the faithful Hanslick said of the C minor that it affected the hearer "as though he read a scientific treatise full of deep philosophical thought." He discovered in it "Faust-like conflicts of the soul," whereas he was cheered by the D major because it hymned "a vernal earth that laughs and blossoms." The D major comforted many who had found the C minor esoteric and severe; though a few were disappointed by the newer work, and made contemptuous remarks about the D major and its "prettiness."

Time, however, has set these two symphonies in a different light for the present generation. The C minor seems to have borrowed something of the rich tenderness, something of the warmly human quality, that was held to be the special property of the D major, and to have conferred upon the latter, in return, something of its own sobriety and depth of feeling. The C minor seems far less austere and much more companionable than it evidently did in 1876, and the D major seems less unqualifiedly a thing merely of "pure happiness and gently tender grace"—though Felix Weingartner rather sourly characterized the Allegretto of the later work as "a graceful trifle almost too insignificant for the other three movements."

But it is the slow movement, with its sombre undertone, that takes the Second Symphony into a region of musical poetry where it keeps company with Brahms at his noblest. There cannot be many who are able to listen without emotion to the opening of this Adagio non troppo—in particular, to that passage where the gravely beautiful melody for the 'cellos weaves about the descending trombone phrase, producing the bitter-sweetness of those moments that dwell in the ear long after the music has passed on to other moods and other spells, like Shelley's enamored wind, "whispering unimaginable things."

❀ ❀ ❀

There are commentators on Brahms who still discuss with solemnity the question whether the D major Symphony is an "idyl"—"Brahms' 'Pastoral' Symphony"; or whether the "undercurrent of tragedy" which they discern in the score takes it out of the class of the innocent, the sunlit, and the "cheerful" in musical art.

Perhaps if we were less eager to put works of art in watertight compartments we should discover that such problems are for the most part imaginary.

Brahms once declared to Clara Schumann that he was "not at all a sensitive person," that he was "absolutely without nerves or sympathy." But it does not require much psychological penetration into the nature of Brahms the man and the artist to make one realize that the reverse was true. Brahms was, in fact, exceptionally sensitive, his nerves were often on the raw, he was acutely sympathetic. The outward Brahms, he of the curt, abrupt, and boorish exterior, was merely the negligible, the protective Brahms—clad, like Jurgen, in "the armor of his hurt."

As an artist it is clear that his sensibility was extreme. He was not only one of those poets who delight in the beauty of the world, who cherish its

[137]

loveliness in their imagination, but he was also one of that lonelier clan who see in living shapes the vesture of decay.

Brahms the pastoral poet, serene in the presence of the loveliness of the created earth, sings out of the D major canticle of the violins near the opening of the first movement, out of the perhaps too facile Allegretto grazioso. We might say that it is the musing and reminiscent Brahms, haunted by the fleetingness of all beloved things, who speaks to us in such a passage as that in the coda of the first movement where the solo horn winds its musing course among the voices of the strings, like "some grave thought threading a dream." But it is Brahms the tragic poet, sensible of those evanescent shapes that are as clouding breaths upon the mirror of the world, who is discernible behind the Adagio non troppo, that profoundest among the slow movements of his symphonies.

Toscanini's manner of setting forth this score unifies all that the music holds and says. It fuses influentially, with unlapsing sensibility and tact, the music's loveliness and brooding gravity. It gives us Brahms the poet of luminous and dreaming solitudes, and Brahms the philosophic agonist, with his deep awareness, somberly compassionate, of the pain and mystery of human life.

SYMPHONY NO. 3, IN F MAJOR

Toscanini achieves a similar art of integration when he sets before us the Brahms of the Third Symphony, in F, so rich in its variety of substance and implication and its changing moods—from the passionate, intrepid opening, to the reconciliatory and decrescent close, with its peace of evening and its still, penumbral loveliness that seems to set the seal of quietness and falling silence upon the heroic striving that has gone before. Toscanini has often played this work for us; but he seems to bring it closer to us with every repetition, as if he had made himself essentially a part of its imaginative being, a living extension of its beauty and its strength.

Brahms completed his Third Symphony in 1883, the year in which Wagner died; and some historians have thought that Brahms may have wished to pay a tribute to his illustrious contemporary when he inserted in the first movement of this symphony, just before the entrance of the second theme, a phrase that recalls the song of the Sirens in the

"Venusberg" scene of *Tannhäuser*. But it may be questioned whether Brahms would have paid his tribute to the dead master in quite that way, involving quite that association of ideas. Certainly the phrase in question does recall the Sirens of *Tannhäuser;* but it is possible that Brahms was unaware of the resemblance. It seems more probable that if he intended in this symphony to pay homage to Wagner's memory, he did so in the solemn and majestic chords for the brass, at the meditative close of the slow movement, which recall the harmonic basis of the noble theme from *Der Ring des Nibelungen* wherewith Wagner portrayed Valhalla, the stronghold of the gods. That, indeed, would have been a fitting tribute from one major deity of music to another.

❀   ❀   ❀

It is interesting to note, by the way, that the Sirens of *Tannhäuser* are not the only beings who have been discovered in this hospitable symphony.

The last movement suggested to Joachim those lovers of Greek legend, Hero and Leander. Joachim thought that the second theme of the Finale, for horn and 'cellos, portrays Leander. Others have been reminded—by the first movement of the symphony at least—of a strikingly different character: Shakespeare's Iago, whose presence in the score appears to have been suggested by the conflict of tonalities that occurs in the opening measures, which seem to express some such underlying dramatic principle as "the bringing together of two opposing forces: Light and Darkness, Good and Evil, Major and Minor."

Thus we see that this symphony has evoked, for different ears and minds, images and moods and characters so fantastically assorted that Alice might almost have dreamed of them in Wonderland. It is more profitable to think of the symphony as music unadorned by "meanings," or only by very general ones: as music in which there is a range of mood and expression exceptional even for Brahms, whose gamut of expressive speech was so wide.

Perhaps he has not elsewhere in his symphonies combined so influentially dramatic power and poetic warmth. The superb opening of the symphony, exhibiting the great theme that descends with so liberal a gesture through the orchestra, is filled with a sweeping, heroic passion of splendid energy and strength. Yet consider, for contrast, the mysterious brooding of those remarkable chords near the end of the Andante, wherein Brahms anticipated by a decade some of the harmonic procedures of a later day. Consider the end of the last movement, with its heart-easing, tranquil dusk and its murmuring quietude. Nowhere in symphonic literature is there a nobler dying of sunset fires, a more magical evocation of outward and of inner peace, than in that luminous descent of the muted strings that brings the work to its assuaging close.

The Brahms of this Third Symphony is not the passionate, dramatic, exultant Brahms of the First Symphony, with its scaling of the sublime, nor the pastoral Brahms of the Second, nor the austerer Brahms of the Fourth. In his Third Symphony, Brahms is by turns passionate and lyric and heroic, as in its companions; but nowhere else in his symphonies has he spoken quite as he has in the last movement of the F major. That slow subsidence of the music at the end into a golden twilight peacefulness, mystically contemplative and serene, is the achievement of a mood that he never elsewhere captured, and it is among the indescribable things of music.

SYMPHONY NO. 4, IN E MINOR

It has often been said that Brahms was fundamentally a sad man; that his inner life, for various reasons, was a tragic one. This supposition does not seem to be borne out by the testimony of some who knew him well. Of course it is true that Brahms experienced the common lot of disappointment, loss, and grief. But apparently he had more reason for being happy than for being sorrowful, and he seems to have realized that fact. A friend who saw much of him through many years has said that Brahms was the happiest man she ever knew; and other friends give similar testimony. But let us remember that a profound philosopher and artist has declared: "Never say you know the last word of any human heart." And that caution applies with special point to those mysterious vehicles of mysterious forces whom we call creative artists.

Probably it is true that no great creative artist is happy in the sense in which most of us use the word. It is also true that happiness and unhappiness are scarcely terms that can properly be applied to men like Beethoven or Brahms or Wagner. It is obvious, as Goethe said, that men of genius work under the compulsion of such extraordinary and exacting conditions, through the mere fact of their being geniuses, that they are debarred from the sort of felicity which ordinary men enjoy. But, in compensation, they experience a kind of happiness that must be almost unbearable in its intensity. Beethoven and Wagner and Brahms agonized over their creative tasks. But that kind of agony is itself a sort of ecstasy. Brahms' biographer and friend, Max Kalbeck, remembered a certain morning when the door of Brahms' workroom stood ajar, and Kalbeck overheard the composer in labor, weeping and groaning in the anguish and ordeal of parturition. On another occasion, he encountered Brahms very early one day, composing by the edge of a forest. Bareheaded and in shirt-sleeves, without collar or cravat, Brahms swung his hat with one hand, while with the other he dragged his coat behind him in the grass. He was hurrying distractedly, as if to escape some invisible pursuer. "Even at a distance," says Kalbeck, "I heard sounds of labored breathing and of moaning. As I approached, I saw his hair hanging down into his face, and the sweat running from it over his hot cheeks. His eyes stared straight forward into emptiness, and gleamed fanatically. He seemed like one possessed. Before I had recovered from my fright, he had shot by me, so close that we almost brushed elbows. I understood at once that it would have been a mistake to address him; for he was burning with the fires of creation. Never shall I forget that sight, and the terrifying impression of elemental force that it made upon me."

That graphic account gives us a glimpse of one of the sources of an artist's devastating rapture. But there must be another and deeper source of happiness peculiar to the creative mind. For when some phrase or melody or movement has achieved its perfect form, the joy of contemplating it must be unique. What it meant to look upon the completed score of the *Eroica,* or the Second Act of *Tristan,* or the F major Symphony, is inconceivable to those who have never experienced the transports and release of imaginative generation—who can never know what it means to be able to bring into being, out of empty space and soundless time, these strange new worlds of beauty and mystery and wonder, created out of nothing, yet a deathless possession thereafter for the solace and the heartenment of men.

❦   ❦   ❦

Brahms was over fifty when he wrote his E minor Symphony. At the time of its composition he was steeping himself in the tragedies of Sophocles, and one of his commentators has said that he transferred their sombreness to the music of this symphony.

Other analysts have found corroborative meaning in the symphony's tonality. According to the worthy Dr. Riemann, Brahms chose the key of E minor because, as Riemann said, "E minor is the tonality of Autumn: it suggests the perishableness of all green and blossoming things." But another critic, referring to this unsuspected secret of Mother Nature, unkindly pointed out that in a symphony by Raff, entitled *In Summer,* the movement which bears the superscription, *A Hot Day,* is, oddly enough, in E minor. And it might be noted that a certain eighteenth century composer asserted that the key of E minor is "akin to the declaration of innocent love."

Brahms of the prickly shell was inwardly, on the whole, an artist who felt acutely the tragedy of human pain—even though he is often in his music gay, serene, content. But whether he remembered Sophocles as he composed this symphony, or believed that the key of E minor is the tonality of Autumn or of Summer, of pessimistic philosophy or of "innocent love," one may not know. But certainly there is little reason to distort the noble gravity and the soberly compassionate melancholy of Brahms the tone-poet into a fundamental depression. To view the E minor Symphony as an utterance of pessimism is to see it in a misleading light. Dejection is hardly its characteristic note. Much of the first movement has a bardic sweep and vigor and heroic power. In the pensive Andante, with its haunting coda, there seems to be no emotion more tragical than a dark-hued, musing, and romantic melancholy. The Scherzo, with its boisterous vigor and its contrasting vein of delicately sportive humor and lyric tenderness, is of course anything but sombre. As for the towering and magnificent Finale, this movement, with its noble severity and strength, gives us an answer, perhaps, to the question whether or not Brahms was essentially a happy man. The answer, it may be, is that he had found something better than happiness: he had found courage. And in the last movement of the E minor he has told us unforgettable things about spiritual valor, and the high gallantry of the brave before those Dark Towers in the paths of men which only the serene and unafraid can dare to meet.

Like other living vehicles of revelation, Toscanini confronts his twentieth performance of a symphony that he would make part of our experience as though he were facing and unveiling it for the first time. He makes us aware of that conviction which inspires every great interpreter: the conviction that, as another of his kind has said, "the voyage of discovery cannot end while the horizon lasts." For him, the gods live endlessly, dust-free and unworn.

This process of disclosure and illumination, of lucid creative synthesis, of reanimating and recreative faith, is in evidence throughout his transference of the E minor Symphony from his experience to ours: in the flowing and large-moulded utterance of the first Allegro; in the sensitive treatment of the Andante; in the gusto and élan of the Scherzo; above all, in the Gothic magnificence of the Finale, where this architect of tone erects before our ears that complex and elusive structure which is but tracery on paper until a master builder quickens it to life.

The stature of the symphony itself, plus the greatness of this reading, combine to stamp in the memories of the responsive an indelible impression of lofty strength and beauty conveyed with an imag-

inative fidelity, a justness and rectitude and eloquence, for which we may well give thanks in a
world where the excellent virtues of the spirit dwell,
as a poet of the past has said, among rocks that are
almost inaccessible, so that a man must wear out his
heart before he can attain them.

Listening to this full-veined and full-voiced
music, so large-moulded and strong and sane, so full
of sap and energy, so splendidly alive, yet so deeply
touched with a sense of the fleetingness of life, it is
difficult to realize that this symphony was once called
sour and ascetic and grim and "weird." Those
epithets are now, of course, grotesquely meaningless
in any such association; they are mere signals of
derogation. Today we listen to the symphonies of
Brahms with a fortified conviction that we are hearing an inspired voice, speaking from an inexhaustible store of beauty and wisdom and understanding,
uttering loveliness and power with the unmistakable
accent of the Gods of the Mountain.

Toscanini's devotion to this music has deepened
immeasurably that conviction. We listen as it issues
from the orchestra through his powers of release.
By what magic of communion, we may wonder, is
he able to share so intimate and deeply right a vision
of these scores with his hundred-odd executants?

[149]

Doubt or believe in, as one chooses, the necromancy of that art of the supreme interpreter which is re-creation, one may not deny that Toscanini has mastered the secret of showing us a known music newly born—rekindled from within.

Perhaps it is as true in the world of the imagination as in the world of the spirit, that, as Blake said, the sun's light when he unfolds it depends on the organ that beholds it; and that it is only those who are uniquely kindled by that unpredictable radiance who can make old veracities flash "like jewels at high noon."

VI

DEBUSSY

A GENERATION ago, when Debussy's symphonic masterpiece, that dazzling evocation of the sea, *La Mer,* was introduced to America, it was rejected by a majority opinion of the critical court as "meaningless rubbish of the dreariest sort." This music, so it was said, contained "more of barnyard cackle" than of the moods and voices of the sea.

That opinion—long since forgotten save by inquisitive prowlers among those catacombs where lie the bones of dead stupidities—must seem preposterous to music lovers of our time. Debussy's *La Mer,* the last of his orchestral works to take its place among the staples of the concert repertoire, has now been recognized for what it is: a matchless flowering of the musical imagination, a work that has not its like in all the literature of music.

In the Spring of 1936, Toscanini conducted in

New York an All-Debussy program. For days the house had been sold out, and long before the concert began the standing-room also was disposed of. The program was heard throughout by a deeply quiet audience; and as piece after piece came to its close, and Debussy's transporting incantations fell into silence, the spellbound listeners seemed to hold their breath until the enchanter had begun again.

Toscanini had elected to end the concert with *La Mer*—apparently unaware that the work had been officially rejected at its American première almost three decades before. The audience, too, seemed unaware: for when the tumultuous evocation reached its close, with Debussy's tonal sunlight blazing upon a sea of lonely and terrifying splendor, while the music flung its cosmic golden shouts across the haunted void, the house, awed for a moment, burst into a clamorous tumult of applause.

Thus do the years redress the balance between an innovating genius and his time; and thus, after a decent interval, does the greatness of exceptional beauty find its place among us as the long night turns to day.

Virtually all Debussy's music is illustrative, in one way or another, of his ability to rouse the inward vision, to express that which is inexpressible. Even in that work of his young manhood, *La Damoiselle Élue,* a setting for women's voices and orchestra of a French version of Rossetti's poem, *The Blessed Damozel,* the mature composer is foreshadowed, and we are made aware of his nascent power of suggestion, his ability to tell us things of which other music had not learned to speak.

Debussy's music for *The Blessed Damozel* has for years been regarded by the average Perfect Debussyite, brought up on *Pelléas* and the *Nocturnes* and *La Mer,* as a very feeble sprouting of the magical Debussyan seed—as music negligibly wan and anemic and unpromising; and the Perfect Debussyites have been inclined to pass it by, their noses in air, and their attention fixed on the authentic wonders of *Pelléas et Mélisande.*

Well, they had better lower their noses, and consider again the music of *The Blessed Damozel,* in the light of Toscanini's disclosure of what the score contains. And while they are about it, they might remember that Debussy began the composition of *Pelléas et Mélisande* only five years after he had completed *The Blessed Damozel.*

Debussy finished *The Blessed Damozel* in 1888, in his twenty-sixth year. When this music was begun (in 1887), Wagner had been dead for only four years, Brahms and Tchaikovsky were still very much alive, and Stravinsky, a boy of five, was riding his velocipede in the suburbs of St. Petersburg. Remembering these facts, one would do well to listen more intently to this remarkable score, in which a new language of expressive tone is eloquently hinted. The music of *The Blessed Damozel,* in comparison with Debussy's later scores, is simple and unadventurous. It has nothing of the prismatic subtlety and the multicolored splendor of *La Mer* or of the *Saint Sebastian* score. Yet *The Blessed Damozel* is an astonishing achievement, beautiful and touching at its best, filled with many premonitions of the master who was to come.

❀   ❀   ❀

Debussy, as a student at Rome in his early twenties, came upon Rossetti's celebrated poem, *The Blessed Damozel,* in the French version by Gabriel Sarrazin, and was captivated by its delicate loveliness and depth of feeling. He finished his music for it after his return to Paris.

It is not strange that he should have been attracted to Rossetti's poem, for there was much in common between the natures of the two artists: Debussy the poetic and mystical composer, and Rossetti the mystical poet.

Dante Gabriel Rossetti, the English poet-painter, whose ancestry was three-fourths Italian, was one of the most variously gifted artists since William Blake, that earlier English master of pictorial and literary art who died the year before Rossetti was born.

Rossetti's genius came to maturity in the fabulous years of the Victorian Age. Among his contemporaries were Browning and Ruskin and Swinburne, Dickens and Tennyson, George Meredith and William Morris, Whistler and Burne-Jones and Carlyle. At the beginning of his career as a painter, Rossetti was one of the Pre-Raphaelites, and for long afterward he was tagged with that opprobrious name. His Pre-Raphaelite affiliations obscured, and still obscure, his essential aesthetic nature. For years he was misunderstood by those dull and bigoted persons who can never see the wood for the trees, and who could not see Rossetti the great and original poet because of the Pre-Raphaelite cult from which he had long before emerged.

The real Rossetti was not the Pre-Raphaelite painter. The real Rossetti was not a painter at all. The real Rossetti was one of the major poets in the English tongue. He died more than half a century ago—while Browning and Tennyson and Ruskin were still alive. Yet his finest poetry is still poetry of the future. Like other rare artistic spirits of the nineteenth century, he is temporarily eclipsed. Probably no one today, save critics and students, reads *The House of Life*—as no one save men of letters reads or knows that other great poetic sequence, the sixteen-line "mock sonnets" of Meredith's *Modern Love* which belong to about the same period as Rossetti's masterpiece. Both are démodé at present. Apparently, they are "cast down deep below the rolling tides of time." Actually, they ride serenely through an unchanging upper sky, obscured, for a while, by low-lying, transient clouds.

Rossetti, in particular, is almost grotesquely out of favor. There is "none so poor to do him reverence." But that fact need not worry those of us who are unaffected by the trends of aesthetic fashion. We shall continue to take down from our library shelves, now and again, Rossetti's nobly impassioned sonnet sequence, *The House of Life,* and, as we read the one called *The Monochord,* that apos-

trophe to the mystical power of music, we may remember what Swinburne wrote of it: that "even
Shelley never expressed the inmost sense and mighty
heart of music as Rossetti has done" in this sonnet.
When we have finished that incomparable sequence
of a hundred and two sonnets, with their splendor
of sound, their sweeping, tumultuous tides of verbal
music and their intensity of imaginative life, we
shall perhaps recall that a sensitive English critic
ranked them as the greatest sonnets in the English
language since those of "the star of poets"—and by
that, of course, he meant Shakespeare.

❁   ❁   ❁

The latter part of Rossetti's life was tragic and
pitiful, filled with bitter remorse and haunted memories and illness and delusions, and a torturing sensibility that would not let him rest. But in his early
years, before his genius and his life took on their
darkly passionate tone, Rossetti, as a youth of nineteen, wrote in 1847 that unique poem which was to
become one of the most famous (and most ridiculed)
in English literature, *The Blessed Damozel*. This
lyric poem has nothing of the depth and passion and
greatness of style that were to mark the sonnets of

The House of Life. Yet *The Blessed Damozel* is poetry of singular tenderness and delicacy of touch, partly narrative, partly reverie and dream and vision.

Rossetti told Hall Caine that he got the idea of his poem from Poe's *Raven.* "I realized," said Rossetti, "that Poe had done the utmost it was possible to do with the grief of the lover on earth; so I determined to reverse the conditions, and give utterance to the yearning of the loved one in heaven." He has handled with exquisite tact this difficult and perilous conception of the cherished woman, the Blessed Damozel, who has died in all the beauty and security and pride of youth, and who awaits in heaven the coming of her lover, who still dwells, disconsolate, on earth.

Rossetti's imagistic daring provoked in its time, of course, the sacred fury of the academics and the delighted howls of the critical gangsters. Yet the sheer imaginative triumph of the thing, its limpid and audacious felicity, still, despite its long familiarity, take one's breath. We follow with compassionate intentness the Blessed Damozel as she leans from the golden barriers of heaven, watching with tears and prayers for some sign of her lover's coming: watching the slow declension of the sun, seeing the curled moon, "like a little feather, fluttering far down the gulf," while she utters her pitiful, impassioned longing—

> "I wish that he were come to me,
> For he will come," she said.
> "Have I not prayed in Heaven?—on earth,
> Lord, Lord, has he not prayed?
> Are not two prayers a perfect strength?
> And shall I feel afraid? . . ."

though at the end, the lover on earth, watching with strained and agonizing gaze, sees the vision fade, the light grow dim, while the groves of Paradise merge into the vague and darkening sky, as the Blessed Damozel casts her arms along the golden barrier, and lays her face between her hands, and weeps.

❀   ❀   ❀

Debussy's setting of Rossetti's poem divides the narrative portions of the text between a chorus of women's voices and the solo voice of a contralto Narrator. The Blessed Damozel herself is a soprano soloist. Debussy omitted ten stanzas of the original text, among them the two finest lines in the poem— which is perhaps just as well: for at that stage of his musical development he could scarcely have set them adequately. Also, he omitted the parenthetical and moving verses in which the lover speaks. Debussy did not conceive the poem in quite the dramatic way that Rossetti did, and so the lover on earth is shut out from the angelic communion of the Blessed Damozel, except as he is reflected to us in her longing and her prayers.

No one but Debussy could have written the music of *La Damoiselle Élue,* with its sensibility and tenderness, its melancholy, rapturous sweetness, its loftiness and purity of mood, its fine-grained beauty, its spiritualized passion.

Behind the brooding and pitiful and prayerful voice of the Blessed Damozel herself we hear, again and again, the utterances of Mélisande—of whom the Damozel is a kind of naïve, angelic sister; and on almost every page there are signs that announce the arrival of a new and unprecedented genius. When the cantata was performed here on Toscanini's Debussy Program, in 1936, and one heard for the first time all that is in the score, one could not doubt that this work was a portent of the mystical and lonely dreamer who was afterward to give us the *Nocturnes* and *Pelléas* and *La Mer,* transforming the music of his time.

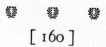

Debussy might have echoed that warning of the character in Maeterlinck's play, *Intérieur:* "Take care! We do not know how far the soul extends beyond man." The strange power and unique intensity of Debussy's art proceed from an acute awareness of the world beyond the senses—the inner life of the imagination, the secret voices of woods and clouds and waters. Like Tristan, he hears "the voice of the light." He is constantly aware of some distant country of the spirit, some shadowy margin of an inaccessible and hidden world—

> . . . The grass beyond the door,
> The sweet keen smell,
> The sighing sound, the lights around the shore.

In the *Nocturnes* for orchestra, *Nuages* ("Clouds"), *Fêtes* ("Festivals"), *Sirènes,* ("Sirens"), he has not attempted to give us tonal impressions of clouds, of festivals, of the ocean's alluring choristers: the music represents an effort to evoke, by indirectness of suggestion, the spiritual counterparts of these things, their reflection in the supersensuous consciousness. It is only upon the borderland of the spirit that he finds what others know as the reality of imaginative experience. In his search for all loveliness that is fugitive and interior and evanescent, he reminds one of the Irishman Yeats; for Debussy is often more Gaelic than Gallic. He is like Yeats in his disdain of those indicative gestures that are merely traditional and apparent, his longing to fix in rhythm and cadence the uncapturable music that haunts his imagination, and the secrets of the world that lies beyond his dreams.

The exquisite reticence of this music, its Mozartean economy of means, should be remarked. With the two clarinets and two bassoons that move across the orchestral canvas at the opening of *Nuages,* and the brief, melancholy plaint of the English horn, Debussy starts the imagination, fills the spiritual eye. In the superb *Fêtes,* with its quivering, iridescent effects of light and color, the most magical of its effects is the most simply accomplished: the sudden pianissimo in the middle of the piece at the suggestion of the distant procession, with the soft throbbing of the harps and timpani and low strings pizzicato, and the three muted trumpets. The gradual approach of the phantom pageant, the dazzling moment of its arrival, and the vanishing of the chimerical revellers in the distance, are achievements of a sort that music had not known before Debussy's day.

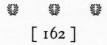

Always, in his typical expressions, Debussy was concerned not with what Maeterlinck contemptuously called "the famous 'real life,'" the outward life, the life we see and hear, but with "that other life which lies at the bottom of men's hearts and in the privacy of their spirits and in the unknown mysteries of this world . . . that life which is silent to our ears, but not to our sympathies." Debussy's most individual achievement was to give us, for the first time in music, a sense of those twilight domains of consciousness, those secret regions of the soul which, as William James tells us, are parted from our normal, waking, rational consciousness by screens of gossamer thinness, but of which most men become aware only through dreams and glimpses. Debussy, having the piercing vision of the mystic, found nothing obscuring in those tenuous screens. His imagination passed into and dwelt at ease in that world beyond the senses; and throughout his life as a creative artist he continued to bring back, from across the border, circumstantial tales of an unknown country—tales of enchanted landscapes and unexplored skies, of fabulous shores where "the noise of the sunfire on the waves at daybreak is audible for those who have ears to hear."

No one had done this before in music; no one

had stood at so remote an outpost of the perceptive mind and reported these mysteriously burdened winds, these tides so incalculably rhythmed, these fantastic and dream-colored landscapes, these murmuring voices of desire, the passionate, grave gestures of these enigmatic actors in some unknowable and hidden drama. This was Debussy's special contribution to creative music. He enlarged the boundaries of its imaginative world, the extent of its awareness, the scope of its expression. He taught it to speak, with unexampled fidelity and beauty and profundity, of many things for which there are no words.

His music is full of those swift and silent intimations that transcend the uttered symbol. It bridges the gulf of human separateness, and, hearing it with sensibility, we have communion with the souls of the living, and, like the visionary of the *Phaedo,* we "see the moon and stars as they really are."

   ✿ ✿ ✿

Among the numerous benefactions for which Euterpe is indebted to Toscanini must be counted his unrewardable services in the cause of Debussy's genius—from the days when he first made *Pelléas et Mélisande* known in Italy, to his first season in America with the Philharmonic, when he began to make us understand *La Mer* in a new and revelatory light.

Before that time, I, for one, had thought that I knew *La Mer*. I had heard its American première in 1907. I had studied the score with diligence and admiration. I had listened to countless performances. But when, for the first time, I heard the work conducted by Toscanini I found that I did not know it at all; that I had never really heard it.

I shall not affront the wondrousness of Toscanini's revelation of Debussy's score by attempting to describe it. It left me, as it left others who also thought they knew *La Mer,* dazed and incoherent and incredulous. We had been listening to *La Mer* in America for almost twenty years before we heard it first from Toscanini: but only then were its images and its voices summoned with plenary power from the wraithlike waters of that phantasmal sea.

He has played the score repeatedly since then, until it has become an integral part of our collective musical consciousness.

❈ ❈ ❈

The score of *La Mer*—those three linked tone-pictures that Debussy called "symphonic sketches" —contains no preface, motto, argument, or explanatory guide except the releasing words that designate the work as a whole, and the subtitles of the different movements: "From Dawn till Noon on the Sea"; "Sport of the Waves"; "Dialogue of the Wind and the Sea."

This music is an incantation; a tonal rendering of colors and odors, of mysterious calls, echoes, visions, imagined or perceived; a recapturing and transcription, through the medium of an art that is consummate sorcery, of "the most fantastical sports of light and of fluid whirlwinds." When Debussy suggests in this music such things as dawn and noon at sea, sport of the waves, gales and surges and far horizons, he is less the poet and painter than the mystical dreamer. It is not chiefly of those familiar aspects of the ocean's winds and waters that he is telling us, but of the changing phases of a sea unknown to mariners or airmen: a sea of strange visions and stranger voices, of fantastic colors and incalculable winds, at times full of bodement and terror, at times sunlit and dazzling. It is a spectacle perceived as in a trance, and evoked by a magician who could summon spirits from the vasty deep.

Yet, beneath these elusive and mysterious overtones, the reality of the sea persists: as we listen, its immemorial fascination lures and enthralls and terrifies; so that we are almost tempted to fancy that the two are, after all, identical: the ocean that seems an actuality of wet winds and tossing spray and inexorable depths and reaches, and that uncharted and haunted and untraversable sea which opens before the magic casements of the dreaming mind.

❦　❦　❦

It is this sea that has been brought close to us by Toscanini—a sea that is shut away from too curious an inspection, to whose murmurs or imperious commands not many have wished or needed to pay heed: a sea both cosmic and jocund, ethereal and tremendous. All this is in Toscanini's performance: a performance that brings the sea about us, swirling through the mind, subduing the senses and the spirit —the sea with its "husky-haughty voice," its timeless fascination, its mystery, and its might.

At one of Toscanini's broadcasts with the NBC Orchestra, he placed *La Mer* upon the same program with the *Pastoral* Symphony of Beethoven. The contrast was daring and illuminative. Both works, as it happens, are evocations of the natural world; yet how utterly different they are in process and effect! One of them, the very sign and symbol of naïve simplicity and candor, a reverent hymn of adoration, profound as it is simple, in praise of the loveliness of the visible and known earth; the other, such an "insubstantial pageant" as Prospero might have dreamt into momentary being—an utterance of the subtlest enchantments of the spirit. Yet Toscanini—who, as Nietzsche said of Wagner, holds dominion over fifty worlds of different ecstasies—passed from one to the other of those disparate regions of the artist's imaginative universe as though he were accomplishing the simplest of feats. Thus is he able to make real for us the visions of those creative dreamers who see existence and the world from separate outposts of the mind.

One thinks of what was said not long ago, prophetically, of Nature and the artist: that we have but to wait, until, with the mark of the gods upon him, there comes among us one who shall continue what has gone before.

VII

SIBELIUS

IT IS heartening to the admirers of Sibelius to reflect that a great and simple artist, in the rich
maturity of his days (the world of music observed
his seventieth birthday on December 8, 1935), may
look back upon his remarkable career with the consciousness that he has invited no meretricious nor
sensational publicity; that, without self-seeking or
self-promotion, he has come at last so magnificently
into his own. In the presence of his art, we know
that we confront the image of one who is, as we
believe, the most independent and detached of living
composers, one who stands aside from the contemporary tonal pageant, watching gravely, as from a
distance, its evolutions and its shows, content to
produce, in quiet and seclusion, the loftiest music of
our time.

He has issued no coin that is not stamped with

his own image. Yet this originality is so seemingly spontaneous, it is achieved by such apparently simple and economical means, that one looks in vain for the secret of its power and distinction. One of his commentators has spoken of his ability to transform and individualize thematic material. And in this respect, as in others, Sibelius is akin to Beethoven. Perhaps the most remarkable of his gifts is this power of revealing a fresh and unsuspected significance in tonal combinations as familiar and accustomed as the morning light—and as mysterious and wonderful. He has always, in varying degree, possessed this power of transforming musical substance into something new and strange.

He can do astonishing things with that simple and at times tremendous musical language that he has developed and perfected. He can speak with grandeur and exaltation and heroic poetry concerning the world about him, concerning that life and nature of which he is peculiarly a part. Sibelius once referred to himself as "a dreamer and poet of Nature." A dreamer and poet he is, beyond dispute. But there are dreamers and dreamers, poets and poets. It is clear that the dreams and the poetry of Sibelius are equally remote from the emotional expansiveness of the Romantics and the iridescent subtleties of those whom some have chosen to call "Impressionists." Sibelius feels the mystery and terror and cruelty of existence too piercingly to sing of it with uncontracted throat; yet he remembers, too, the greatness of man's unconquerable will.

❦   ❦   ❦

One salutes him as a creator who in his own lifetime has become a classic: as a composer whose music already possesses that unmistakable quality which tells us that we are in the presence of something that has no temporal bounds, that is neither old nor new, that is unaffected by the trends of aesthetic fashion or the desire for novelty or sensation or acclaim.

When we look back over the remarkable succession of great works produced by Sibelius during his long creative life, especially his seven [1] epoch-making symphonies, we are stirred by the realization that this is music of the rarest nobility and strength, marked by an aesthetic integrity above suspicion and without a flaw.

There is present in this music a blend of passion

[1] Sibelius is said, at this date, to be working upon his Eighth Symphony.

and austere restraint that sets it apart among the productions of our time. It possesses an intensity that is mastered and controlled, lending its hearers something of its own security and command. Its moods and emotions do not lie upon its surface. They are veiled behind that expressive economy of speech which adds so immeasurably to its eloquence. One returns to the art of Sibelius again and again; chiefly, perhaps, because one finds in it sources and currents of unfailing strength. There is something oddly fortifying in the air and the winds of those high places that his musical thought inhabits—something that at times is astringent and severe, something that challenges and tests and cures.

❦   ❦   ❦

The processes of this music are inscrutable, as Nature is inscrutable. Their inscrutability is part of their inner life and movement; it is of their essence. The thoughts of Sibelius the artist move on the far side of an indefinite boundary. They move as those who go upon a secret errand. They are shut away from us by the very clarity and simplicity that deceptively surround them. We reach toward them, and they have moved away, beyond our grasp. Their very directness is a cloak, and we shall probably never know quite what they would say to us, or why they haunt and stir us as they do, or why they have added a new significance and a new dimension to the world of the musical imagination.

The art of Sibelius has the reticence of the strong, the mysteriousness of the simple. We listen to what a profound and withdrawn spirit, a poet and philosopher in tones, has chosen to tell us of his vision of Nature and of human life. We are unaccountably moved by what he says to us. He has restored our faith in the capacity of great music to renew itself from age to age, from period to period. We know, now, that symphonic genius did not die with a generation that is past. We know that it lives on in Sibelius, exhaustless in strength and beauty and significance, charged with that old, immortal power which tells us that another master dwells among us.

❁ ❁ ❁

How often, in recent years, an orchestral concert has reached its apex in a performance of music by Sibelius—especially when Toscanini has stood before it and within it! One must rank among the most powerful impressions made by Toscanini during his inaugural season with the NBC his achievement with the heroic Second Symphony of Sibelius. Toscanini had not previously conducted that unsettling score—though his relation of what Sibelius has to say in his Fourth Symphony remained an indelible memory.

The Second Symphony has been the bane of those who would explain in words its "meaning." When the eminent Finnish conductor, Georg Schneevoigt, an intimate friend of Sibelius, was in America as guest conductor of the Boston Symphony Orchestra in 1924, he made the statement that Sibelius in this symphony intended to depict in the first movement "the quiet, pastoral life of the Finns undisturbed by thought of oppression." The second movement, he said, is charged with patriotic feeling, "but the thought of a brutal rule over the people brings with it timidity of soul." The third movement, in the nature of a scherzo, "portrays the awakening of national feeling, the desire of the Finns to organize in defense of their rights"; while in the finale, "hope enters their breasts, and there is comfort in the anticipated coming of a deliverer."

The late Ferruccio Busoni, who also had been

a friend of the composer's, thought quite differently. "Sibelius," he wrote in his *Von der Einheit der Musik*, "may be thought of as the Finnish Schubert [hardly the most felicitous of comparisons!]. The folk-ways of his country," Busoni continued, "flow directly from his heart to his pen. The Second Symphony consists of a spring-like first movement concealing many unopened buds, a slow movement unfolding the full maturity of late summer, and a scherzo which merges into the finale, where at last the Finnish earth breaks into its own song."

❦　❦　❦

But alas for "inspired" explanations! Sibelius himself does not seem to have known anything about these things. If the scherzo of the Second Symphony portrays, as Mr. Schneevoigt said that it does, "the desire of the Finns to organize in defense of their rights"; if the first movement conceals, as the more lyrical Busoni declared, "many unopened buds," this knowledge appears to have been withheld from Sibelius. For in an interview that he gave at London he declared brusquely: "My symphonies are music conceived and worked out in terms of music, and without any literary basis."

[175]

That is the worst of ascribing "programs" to music, even if first-rate musicians like Busoni contrive them; or even if they proceed from the composer himself. "All music," said Whitman, "is what awakes from you when you are reminded by the instruments."

What awakes from some listeners when they are reminded by the instruments is generally a picture of some sort. What awakes in those of sensitive responsiveness is something that is continuous with the music itself, woven of its own substance: something that fulfills and completes, something with which words can have no commerce save by analogy and image—something whose identity depends upon the subtlest and most complex interaction between the music and the listener's brain and nerves. The more sensitive the interchange, the less communicable the result—except in terms of the music's own language.

❦　❦　❦

It is among the most remarkable of Toscanini's powers that he is able, in a degree unmatched by other interpreting musicians, to evoke and maintain in the listener's imagination this sense of identity and continuity with the essence of the music that is being played. There is no phase of the interpreter's art that is less explicable; and none that is more immediately to be felt and recognized by the responsive.

The inaccessibility that is characteristic of Sibelius's thought, the subtle simplicities of its musical texture, seem to have awaited, for their full conveyance, the special faculties that Toscanini brings to all his undertakings. The Second Symphony of Sibelius had been played repeatedly in America; yet to some of us it seemed that, for the first time, we found ourselves face to face with the Sibelius who lives behind the surface of this music.

And in all the years that Toscanini has been among us, achieving triumph after triumph of eloquent identification with great music, I cannot remember that he had ever surpassed the exhibition of sustained intensity and cumulative power with which he and his coöperative orchestra evolved that long crescendo of heroic power and heroic exaltation which Sibelius has spread over an entire symphony.

Once again, on that occasion, old faiths, and new, were verified.

VIII

FROM WAGNER'S TREASURY

WHETHER Wagner's music is closer to Toscanini's secret heart than any other, it is not
possible to say. But certainly he possesses a mastery
of its style and a profound identification with its
quality that have long seemed his alone.

Wagner is all about us. Day in and day out we
hear his music—that music which stirs uniquely the
layman and the listening novice, and fills with incredulous amazement those connoisseurs and students who think they know it best.

How inviting and accessible this music looks to
the average interpreter, with its relatively simple
rhythms, its great tunes that have long since sung
themselves into the ears and imaginations of the
world, its nobility and tenderness and passion, its
eloquence that seems so easily releasable—this music
that almost plays itself! Yet when we test the aver-

age performance of a Wagner score by the touch-
stone of our conception of its ideal delivery, by the
standard of the music's inherent possibilities, we
know that we have been deluding ourselves with
substitutes and makeshifts, and that what we hear
is seldom a complete account of what is there.

❧   ❧   ❧

Toscanini does with Wagner's music what he
does with other music: which is to remind us that
the truth about a masterwork is infinitely stranger
than the commonplace fictions that lesser interpreters weave about its greatness; that the treasures of
beauty and significance in great music are more
abundant than we had dared to think; and that the
heavens of the re-creative mind may still declare the
glory of whatever gods there be.

Toscanini's conducting of Wagner's music,
here and abroad, has always left in the minds of the
susceptible the same unshakable conviction: that this
was Wagner's music as he himself had dared to
dream that it might sound.

What Wagner said of the probable effect of
Tristan is true of all his greater music: that fine
performances of it would be intolerable—"they

would be forbidden," he wrote. "Nothing but indifferent performances can save me!" Poor Wagner
was often, in his own time, "saved" in just that way;
and many of us today are often saved from the
effect of that which makes this music, at its greatest,
insupportable. But we are helpless when it is such
an interpreter as Toscanini who applies himself to
the conveyance of pages from *Tristan,* or *Walküre,*
or *Götterdämmerung,* or *Parsifal.* There is nothing,
then, to intervene between the impact of Wagner's
genius at its most unbearable and the sensibilities
of the responsive; and we find ourselves almost inclined to echo Wagner's prophecy, and to hope for
the application of his remedy.

❀   ❀   ❀

It would be vain to attempt a recital of Toscanini's deeds of restoration in the playing of Wagner's scores: for one would find oneself undertaking
a measure-by-measure listing of achievements.

Restoration is, I think, the justly descriptive
word. For what Toscanini does with this music is to
render unto Wagner that which is Wagner's.

In the First Act of *Die Walküre,* for example,

most of us have heard innumerable times that affecting recurrence of the Valhalla theme in the strings and wind at Sieglinde's words to Siegmund concerning that mysterious Stranger who had left his sword in the ashtree's trunk for the hero who could draw it forth: "Then knew I who it was who in sorrow greeted me." We have heard the refulgent climax of the orchestra as Siegmund plucks from the ashtree's stem the predestined sword of Wotan, and shows it to the enraptured Sieglinde; we have listened, time and again, to the frenzied postlude that accompanies and follows the closing of the curtains at the end of the Act as the insensate pair embrace, and Wagner's orchestra goes mad with exultation. But when have these things sounded with such conquering fidelity as they do when Toscanini draws them forth—the mystery and awe and tenderness of the Valhalla passage; the jubilant blazing of the sword theme through the orchestra at the moment of Siegmund's triumph; the delirium of the instruments as the lovers fall into each other's arms?

When Toscanini plays this music, and the music of daybreak from the *Götterdämmerung* Prologue, and the death scene of Siegfried, and the opera's fiery epilogue, while the orchestra exults and mourns and prophesies and turns the heavens into sacrificial flame, we are aware beyond doubt or peradventure that we have heard the living voice of Wagner. And we tell ourselves, in wonderment, "But this is not the *Götterdämmerung* we knew!" It is not, indeed. Yet the conviction persists that it is the *Götterdämmerung* that Wagner knew—or rather the *Götterdämmerung* that he conceived. And this is true of all the music by Wagner that Toscanini plays.

❀ ❀ ❀

What Toscanini gives us, then, is the completeness of the music's truth—no more, no less. Just how that truth is apprehended and conveyed one may not know; and yet one may conjecture.

It was Wagner himself who said, with curtness and profundity, that "music is unseizable except through song." Wagner the thinker was a civilized internationalist; yet the truth that he stated is not merely a secret bound up with the Italian conception of music as essential song. It is fundamentally a musical secret. It is the key that unlocks not only the inner heart of a concerto by Vivaldi, but of an aria by Handel or Bach or Mozart, a symphony by Beethoven or by Brahms, or an Act of *Götterdämmerung*.

[182]

That truth is one that Toscanini has not had to learn. Instinctively and always, in playing Wagner, he pursues the *melos,* the melodic principle, into every depth and height and extremity, every detail and ornament, of the tonal structure. He finds it in figurations and in an inner voice; in the intervals between great moments, and in the mightiest of those moments themselves, when the shape and impetus of Wagner's huge design bear the music to its heights. And always the beauty and sensibility of phrasing, the poetic penetration, the instant responsiveness to the shape and contour of the musical thought, are final and consummate.

Lyricism, in the special sense of the word, is only one of the many phases of this captured *melos.* Its home and special haunt is music of spiritual contemplation, of impassioned reverie and self-communion. Yet Toscanini reminds us that song and drama interpenetrate; and his own excelling gift is that of blending beauty with vitality, loveliness with strength. He is the unapproachable magician of orchestral song: yet there is no such master of rhythm, of heroic and dramatic evocation; no such architect of climax: his crescendi shake the spirit by their inexorable sweep and power and momentum. Yet in

all the fury of his cumulative ardors he never ceases
to be musical.

❦ ❦ ❦

This astonishing artist recalls to us many say-
ings of the wise that illuminate the mastery which
he exerts. That mystical realist, William Blake, declared that "the enormous and the minute are inter-
changeable manifestations of the Eternal which is
always present to the wise." Blake himself gave us
innumerable disclosures of immensity; and long before Science, with a startled gasp, discovered that
the mystics of the world have always been its pioneer
tellers of realistic truth, he was aware that little-
ness is a delusion of materialistic minds—though he
did not know that in the atom are unbridgeable
gulfs through which the particles swing like suns.

Toscanini is one of those artists who confirm
the incredible realities of mystical truth. Again and
again, in his interpretations, he proves to us that the
minute may become enormous—enormous in value
and significance.

Consider, as one among the countless felicities
of expressive detail that he achieves, his treatment
of the little three-note phrase for the clarinet which,
in the concert version of the "Good Friday Spell,"

joins the middle section in B major with the final
section in D. This is only, to the casual eye, connec-
tive tissue. But Toscanini's eye is not casual. It is
probing and revelatory. How often has one heard
that inconspicuous little phrase played as if it were
a mere incident in the unfolding of the movement!
Yet Toscanini shows us, by an infallible rightness
of phrasing and articulation, that not even transi-
tional material, used to bridge a gap in an abbrevi-
ated score, need be lifeless and inutile. He makes the
small phrase a subtle preparation for the great one
that is to follow it, so that it becomes an essential
part of the fabric of the music, and is caught up
into the beauty and sadness that encompass it, like
some almost inaudible sigh of immemorial grief aris-
ing from the veiled and muted orchestra.

❀   ❀   ❀

It may be that only those who have heard Toscanini conduct the music of Wagner over a period
of many years can be fully aware of his inexhaustibly renewed intensity. Long ago he was transcendent. What he is today can scarcely be affirmed without apparent overemphasis: for no praise of his
ability to realize an ideal image could possibly be

just without seeming also to be extravagant in the estimation of the unresponsive. But for those who listen with susceptibility, what must it mean to hear for the first time, as performed by such a minister, such music as the Prelude to *Lohengrin,* or the Prelude and Good Friday scene from *Parsifal,* or the music of the dawn that breaks upon the parting of Siegfried from Brünnhilde—what a process of exaltation and release, and what an unappraisable experience!

If it be true, as Nietzsche remarks in *The Birth of Tragedy,* that "it is only as an aesthetic phenomenon that existence and the world are eternally justified," then it might be said that music-making such as this can bring us measurably nearer to that eminence whence we shall see that possibly, after all, the world is well designed.

On Toscanini's programs are works that have been endlessly exploited. Yes, one has heard this Wagner music many times, from many hands. And then one listens to it under Toscanini and hears the great phrases of Siegfried's Funeral Hymn sung with the sorrowful sublimity that is their proper voice; hears the ineffable tenderness of the Good Friday music issue like an exhalation from the orchestra; hears again the pauses between the open-

[186]

ing phrases of the *Tristan* Prelude made articulate
with longing and despair; hears the closing measures of the Liebestod shaped and spaced like mobile
sculpture, and edged with the sunset fires of that
unearthly dusk.

❦ ❦ ❦

Hearing thus, I remembered what a wise and
sensitive friend had said to me not long since—
that "the inner life no longer exists: that many of
those who talk religion today mean nothing more
than better treatment of their fellow men and higher
ideals of social justice. Great experience, creative
impulse, quickening, are things that scarcely count."

And yet they count increasingly, after all: they
are part of what we mean today by beauty and greatness and exalted truth.

IX

THE MUSIC LOVER

WHAT is it that Toscanini chiefly means to those who cherish and revere him?

He is first of all and obviously, of course, a genius, and a consummate craftsman. But there are many geniuses, many consummate craftsmen. When you have the craftsman of genius plus the fanatically pure of heart, the dedicated celebrant, you have the phenomenon that is Toscanini.

It was a modern artist of exquisite authenticity and profound discernment, the late Katherine Mansfield, who observed that "one reason for the poverty of art today is that artists have no religion. . . . For artists," she added, "are priests after all." With few exceptions, the greatest creative artists, at least in music, have been religious—not in the narrow and doctrinal sense of the word, but in its free and ultimate and sublimating sense. Today, is it not rather the great interpreters who are religious in that unconfined and ultimate and dedicatory sense— is it not to them that the custody of the Grail has passed? Is it not they, the few who are truly consecrated and elect, the priests and guardians of immortal beauty, who are filled with that mystical power of creative faith which can turn an act of service into a miracle of resurrection?

Who of us can forget the fathomless serenity, the rapt loveliness of mood and pace and accent, that Toscanini draws from the slow movement of the Ninth Symphony? Or the epic mourning of the Dirge from *Götterdämmerung?* Or the magically recovered innocence of the *Pastoral* Symphony? Or the startling glory of the music of the resurrection in the *Missa Solemnis?* Hearing such feats of realization, one knows what it means when an artist of piercing and creative vision sets himself to this task of imaginative identification and fulfillment: when the interpreter becomes merged with that which is interpreted. We seem to be listening for the first time to the essential reality that lies behind the music, so that we find ourselves saying, in amazement: "This *is* the dreamer rapt and transfigured; this *is* the mourning voice of heroes; this *is* the wisdom of the hills and of sunlight and quiet valleys and free winds; this *is* the glory of the risen dead gathered up to Paradise."

♣   ♣   ♣

One cannot say that such things are the issue of genius alone: for many of those artists who transmit music eloquently to the listener have indisputable genius, yet lack that mysterious quality which makes a Toscanini what he is. Perhaps it has nothing essentially to do with genius—though the rare interpreter cannot, of course, dispense with genius, any more than the inspired prophet can dispense with speech, though it is not in speech that his prophetic power lies.

Given, then, the interpreter of genius, what is it that must be added in order to set him among those transcendent and lonely artists who appear but once or twice in a generation, and whom we recognize at once as chosen and apart? Is it aesthetic integrity? Or humility? Or selflessness? Or completeness of dedication? Or intensity of belief? Or faith? Or is it a kind of love—a love so incandescent and transforming that the one possessed of it reminds us of that luminous, enraptured being of whom Dante speaks as "enamored, so that he seems made of fire"?

Perhaps it is no one of these qualities, but all
of them, that must be added to the artist of genius
before he is fit to stand with the elect; for the sum
of them is unqualified devotion, a kind of worship;
and that, it may be, gives us a hint of the truth. We
shall find, I think, that the supreme interpreter is
not commanding music: instead, it is commanding
him—filling him with a divine humility, a divine ecstasy of revelation, a divine excess of love.

Of all the musicians one has observed and
studied as interpretative artists, there has been none
who loved music with the undivided intensity that
is characteristic of Toscanini. As Shelley, one might
say, is the perfect type of the poet, the poet *in excelsis,* so Toscanini is the music lover *in excelsis.*

Toscanini has many qualities as an interpreting
musician. But the one that integrates them all is a
passion for music so imperious and ungovernable
that it will not let him rest until he has shared with
us, through the medium of the instruments that he
commands and inspires, his image of the ideal beauty
that possesses him.

A scholastic philosopher of an earlier century
said that the influence of inspired men is to be explained in four ways. First, he said, because they
have an undistorted vision of reality. Second, be-

cause they are receptacles of light. Third, because they know, and make us know, that the reality which they perceive is identical with beauty. Fourth, because they are distinguished by what he called "an excess of love," which is "an inextinguishable radiance, illuminating others."

I think that this describes all men, all artists, who are vehicles of what we call, for want of a better name, inspiration. Their perception is undistorted; they receive illumination; they see beauty as the supreme reality of the spirit; and their love of it is boundless, irradiating, and creative.

※ ※ ※

That supreme quality of love belongs to the greatest re-creative artists. Yet it is shared in humbler measure by all those of us for whom music is indispensable. I have sometimes wondered what proportion of those whom we call music lovers would come within this classification. Are they relatively few, or relatively many, those to whom music is indispensable?

For many persons, music is only an amenity, something to which one resorts after the crossword puzzle has been solved and other diversions are exhausted. That is one way of enjoying music. There is another way, which one might illustrate by quoting the apocryphal remarks of Lucullus to Caesar on the subject of music, as they are found in Landor's brilliant collection of character studies called *Imaginary Conversations*.

This is Lucullus speaking:

"I listen to music willingly at all times, but most willingly while I am reading. At such times, a voice or even a whisper disturbs me: but music refreshes my brain when I have read long. I find also that if I write poetry, listening to music gives rapidity and variety and brightness to my ideas. Sometimes, I command a fresh instrument or another voice; which is to the mind like a change of posture or of air to the body. My health is benefited by the gentle play of sounds thus opened to the most delicate of the fibres."

❁   ❁   ❁

Well, that way of listening to music has its merit, and no one need say a word against it. But it is a way that implies the use of music as a means, as an aid to something else—an aid to thinking, or daydreaming, or relaxing, or recuperating. It is not the way of the music lover. It is not the way of those who are possessed by music, either as listeners or as interpreters. For them, music is something imperious and tyrannical—not soothing, not refreshing, not diverting; but often exhausting and almost unendurable, as terrible as flame or revelation. But always it possesses.

We sometimes say of a friend or an acquaintance, "He is passionately fond of music." Is he? The pertinent question has been asked, "What will he do for it? Will he forgo leisure, forget to eat, face poverty? Will the blood leave his face as he listens to the Third *Leonore* Overture or the Finale of Schubert's C major Symphony?" That is a fair question and a searching one.

In Karel Capek's inimitable book, *The Gardener's Year,* one may read about the kind of lover that I have in mind: one for whom the thing he loves is despotic and possessing—though the object of Capek's love is not music, but a garden.

"I will tell you," writes Capek, "how to recognize a true gardener."

" 'You must come to see me,' he says: 'I will show you my garden.' Then, when you go (just to please him), you will find him busy somewhere among the perennials. 'I will come in a moment,' he shouts to you, over his shoulder. 'Just wait till I have planted this rose.'

" 'Please don't worry,' you say kindly to him.

"After a while he must have planted it; for he gets up, shakes your hand, and covers it with damp earth. Then, beaming with hospitality, he says: 'Come and have a look: It's a small garden, but— wait a moment!' and he bends over a bed to weed some tiny grass. 'Come along. I will show you my Dianthus Musalae—it will open your eyes . . . Great Scott! I forgot to loosen it here!' he says, and begins to poke in the soil, forgetting you entirely.

"A quarter of an hour later he straightens up again. 'Ah!' he says, 'I wanted to show you that bellflower, Campanula Wilsonae. That is the best campanula which— Wait a moment! I must tie up this delphinium.'

"After he has tied it up, he remembers: 'Oh, I see, you have come to look at that erodium. Just a moment!' he murmurs. 'I must transplant this aster; it hasn't enough room here!'

"After that, you go away on tiptoe, leaving him absorbed among the perennials.

"When you meet him again, he will say: 'You must come to see me; I have one rose in flower, a

pernetiana; you have not seen that before. Will you
come? Do!'

"Very well; you will go and see him again as
the year passes by, when you have plenty of time.
Meanwhile, you depart, leaving the gardener to his
inexhaustible desires."

That is Capek's picture of his equivalent of the
music lover, the insatiable gardener. It helps us, I
think, to recognize that cultivator of spiritual soils
and seeds to whom music is indispensable. We shall
know what music means in his life by the degree
to which it possesses him. The test is as simple and
as certain as that. We shall find that the music lover
is not commanding music, after the manner of
Lucullus, for his benefit and ease. Instead, music
is commanding him, wreaking itself upon him, and
—if he be one of the elect among its ministers—filling him with an impassioned humility and devoutness, a consuming ecstasy of revelation, a divine excess of love. If he be artist and music lover at once,
we shall recognize that he must perforce achieve his
act of re-creation in his own image; and we can but
repeat the wondering words of Dante as he saw in

Beatrice's eyes the changing image of the Truth un-
changed:

> ". . . within myself I marvelled,
> When I beheld the thing itself stand still,
> And in its image it transformed itself."

We shall realize that the artist, this music lover
in excelsis, is continually refreshed with the waters
of that living fountain of Dante's Everlasting Garden; and that he has become, like every human instrument of a beauty passionately understood, part
of that radiant energy "which moves the sun and
the other stars."

❧   ❧   ❧

Toscanini is that kind of music lover. Music
is unspeakably dear to him, a wonderful and sacred
thing; and by some mysterious and inexplicable
power of communication he makes it so for those
of us who also love and cherish it.

A poet has told us that the truth and rapture
of man are holy things, not lightly to be scorned.
Toscanini is constantly reminding us that this holiness of the truth and rapture of man exists in the
memorials of created art. His sense of the inviolabil-
ity of great music, the priestly quality of his attitude

toward its revelation, will always remain, for those who have been aware of them, among the major validations of one's occasionally wavering belief that man is worthy of the stewardship of everlasting things.

"The Golden Age had not its name from those who lived in it," remarked Dr. Burney somewhat caustically many years ago. There are several things less likely than that musical historians of the future will give that name to the age in which Toscanini once wrought his miracles of transubstantiating beauty, in the presence of awed believers who can no longer tell of them only because they have fallen silent among the forgotten, happy dead.

Now and again, unpredictably, in the course of the generations, an artist such as this appears—some rare and luminous apparition emerges out of time and space, burns for a while with valor and swift flame among the chaos and the murk, and finally departs, leaving untarnishable memories. Those moments are of inestimable price, for it is then that the content of life seems fullest and most rich—as when we meet "the friend of friends," or pause suddenly, face to face with beauty, and know that life, for all its frustration and its treachery, is full of wonder, beneficence, and grace.

INDEX

INDEX

INDEX

INDEX

Shaw, George Bernard, 17
Shelley, Percy Bysshe, 136, 157, 191
Sibelius, Jean, 33, 169-175, 177
Sirènes ("Sirens"), Debussy, 161
Sophocles, 146
Spohr, Ludwig, 78-79
Stadler, Abbé, 85
St. Petersburg, 154
Stravinsky, Igor, 154
Sturm, 70
Sullivan, J. W. N., x, 65
Surprise Symphony, Haydn, 37
Swinburne, Charles A., 155, 157
Symphonies:
  Beethoven:
    First, 37, 90
    Third (see *Eroica*)
    Fifth, in C minor, 15-16, 43, 47, 60-62, 64-68
    Sixth (see *Pastoral*)
    Seventh, 44, 71, 77-80, 82-88
    Ninth, 17, 25, 43, 47-48, 57, 66, 74, 88-90, 92, 94-100, 103-105, 107, 111, 123, 127, 134, 189
  Brahms:
    First, in C minor, 123, 126-127, 128-129, 132, 135-136, 142
    Second, in D major, 136, 142
    Third, in F major, 139, 142, 145
    Fourth, in E minor, 142-143, 146-148
  Haydn:
    B-flat major, 34
    G major, 34-35, 40
  Mozart:
    C major, 36
    E-flat, 36
    G minor, 36
  Schubert:
    C major, 116, 121-122, 127, 194
  Sibelius:
    Second, 174-175, 177
    Fourth, 174
    Eighth, 171

Tannhäuser, Wagner, 140
Teetgen, Alexander, 85
Tennyson, Alfred, Lord, 155-156
Thalberg, Sigismund, 92
Thayer, Alexander Wheelock, x, 52, 61, 71, 98
Thomas, Ambroise, 26
Thompson, Francis, 122
Thoreau, Henry, 14, 75
Toscanini, Arturo, *passim*
Tovey, Sir Donald, x, 50, 99
Tristan, Wagner, 28, 44, 96, 145, 179-180, 187
Tschaikovsky, Piotr, 125, 154
Tuileries Palace, 35

Umlauf, Michael, 92-93
Unger, Karoline, 93
Unger, Max, 96
United States, 6, 7, 35
Upanishads, 104

Vallombrosan Symphonies, Haydn, 36
Victorian Age, 155
Vienna, 61, 67, 78, 83, 90, 119, 126
  University of, 78
Villette, Giroud de, 36
Vivaldi, Antonio, 38, 182

Wagner, Richard, 16, 18, 23-24, 28, 31, 33, 37, 44-45, 49, 81, 83-84, 89, 139-140, 143-144, 154, 168, 178-180, 182-183, 185-186
Wagner, Siegfried, 83
Walküre, Die, Wagner, 180
Weber, Carl Maria von, 73, 78
Weingartner, Felix, 50, 136
Whistler, James Abbott McNeill, 155
Whitman, Walt, 129, 176
Winged Victory, 122
Winterreise, Schubert, 119
Wordsworth, William, 3, 127

Yeats, William Butler, 162

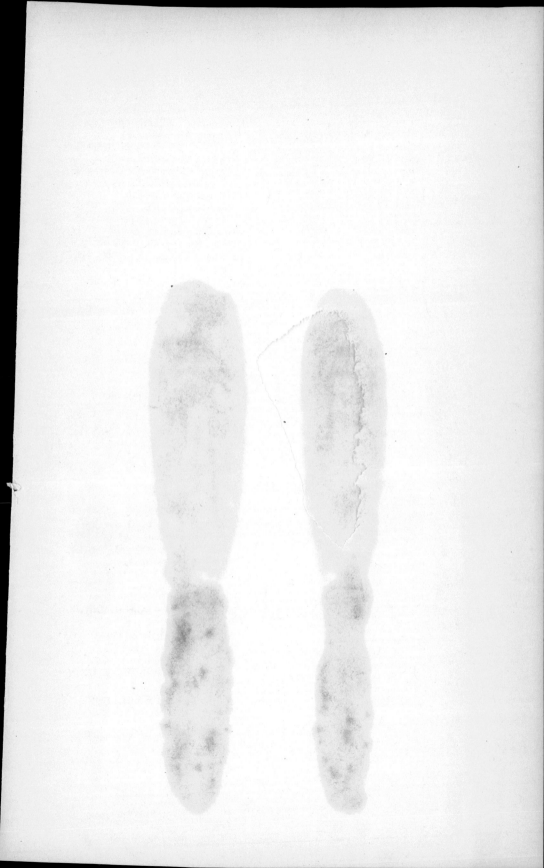